Antique Biedermeier Furniture

Antique Biedermeier Furniture

Rudolf Pressler, Stefan Döbner, Wolfgang L. Eller

4880 Lower Valley Road, Atglen, PA 19310 USA

Special thanks for her cooperation on this book to Frau Beatrix Empl.

Dimensions are given in centimeters, height x width x depth.

Originally published as *Biedermeier Möbe*l, *Antiquitten-Katalog* by Verlag Battenberg, München, 2001.
Translated from German by Edward Force.

Title page illustration: Chair, one of four, Vienna, circa 1815, mahogany, maple, with watercolor painting. $15,000-17,000.
Half title page illustration: A fancy armchair, Regensburg, circa 1805, see catalog no. 449, p. 218.

Layout by Bonnie M. Hensley
Typeset in Dutch801 Rm BT

ISBN: 0-7643-1648-6
1 2 3 4

Published by Schiffer Publishing Ltd.
4880 Lower Valley Road
Atglen, PA 19310
Phone: (610) 593-1777; Fax: (610) 593-2002
E-mail: Schifferbk@aol.com
Please visit our web site catalog at **www.schifferbooks.com**

In Europe, Schiffer books are distributed by Bushwood Books
6 Marksbury Avenue Kew Gardens
Surrey TW9 4JF England
Phone: 44 (0) 20-8392-8585; Fax: 44 (0) 20-8392-9876
E-mail: Bushwd@aol.com
Free postage in the UK. Europe: air mail at cost.

This book may be purchased from the publisher.
Include $3.95 for shipping. Please try your bookstore first.
We are always looking for people to write books on new and related subjects.
If you have an idea for a book please contact us at the above address.
You may write for a free catalog.

Contents

Preface 7
Introduction 8

The Biedermeier Era

Biedermeier as an Artistic and Cultural Concept 11
Political Restoration and Withdrawal into Privacy 11
Living Conditions at the Beginning of the 19th Century 12
Progress After the Founding of the German   Customs Union 12
The Bourgeois Homeowner 13
The Bourgeois Family's Everyday Life 14
A Change Begins to Develop 14

The Furniture Style

Origin, Creation, Features 15
Rediscovering the Antique 15
British Models: Late Rococo 15
"Good Taste" Prevails 16
Regional Differences 16
Technical Innovations 17
Developments and Tendencies and Free Formation in Late Biedermeier 18
Temporal Parallels: Late Empire and Biedermeier 18
Obsolescence and Rediscovery of Biedermeier Style 19

Furniture Types

Bureaus and Writing Desks 20
Cupboards, Cases and Chests 21
Tables 21
Small Furniture 22
Chairs and Couches 22
Beds 23
Other Furniture 23

Furniture Designs

Appearance 24
Placing Furinture in Rooms, Woodworking Techniques, Design 24
Cubic Designs and Decor Elements 28
Mechanical Developments: Metal Fittings 29

Furniture Areas and Centers

Vienna, Austria, Bohemia and Hungary 31
Bavaria and Franconia 33
Baden and Württemberg 34

Mainz and Hesse 34
Saxony and Thuringia 34
Berlin 35
Pomerania and East Prussia 36
North Germany 36
The Rhineland 37

Maintaining Value by Restoration and Care

Types of Damage 38
Preservation 39
       Protection from Vermin 39
       Preservation of Structural Elements and Finishes 40
       Preservation of the Wood Surfaces 40
       Proper Maintenance Protects Against Damage 42
       How to Avoid Damage 42
Restoration 43
       Dealing with Bad Spots 43
       Repairing Wood Breakage 43
       Replacement of Missing Parts 44
       Veneer Damage 44

Tips, Trends and Market Tendencies 46

Catalog Illustration Section

Notes on the Catalog Section and Price Guide 47
Furniture Trademarks 48
Color Section 49
Bureaus 82
Chiffoniers and Chests 103
Writing Cabinets 110
Writing Bureaus 114
Cupboards 146
Bookcases and Showcases 168
Tables 178
Writing Desks and Secretaries 194
Chairs 202
Armchairs 216
Couches 222
Benches 234
Wing Chairs 235
Etageres 236
Small Furniture and Other Items 238
Mirrors 240

Appendix

Glossary 244
Bibliography 252
Photo Credits 254
Directory of Dealers 256

Preface

Biedermeier furniture enjoys lasting appreciation. With its high functionality and simple, uncomplicated forms, it suits today's modern sense of living. This appreciation corresponds with the great demand for up-to-date information on this style of furniture.

In the text, the recent research, especially that of the last decade, is included and amplifies the considerable contributions of the previous studies. This refers in particular to the characterization of Biedermeier not as a typically bourgeois style, but one with aristocratic origins, which likewise found widespread popularity among the well-to-do upper middle class.

In the large illustrated section, the furniture types are grouped in a more comprehensible manner and ordered regionally as well as chronologically. The regional differences of the types are therefore easier to comprehend. A balance between the various furniture regions could, it is true, not be achieved completely, yet typical pieces from all regions have been illustrated. The color illustrations in the book have been upgraded by new and special examples from the present-day market.

The origins of the furniture could be dated more exactly thanks to the results of research in the most recent years, especially the great Biedermeier expositions in Munich and Vienna. Early "Proto-Biedermeier" pieces have been better represented, as have regional delays. The datings of the later style have been differentiated more strongly as to their times of origin.

The price guide is suited to the present-day market.

Sofa, Vienna, circa 1820.

Introduction

Another furniture book in this series of "antique catalogs"? many will ask skeptically, or: Another book about Biedermeier furniture? Yet even a quick look through the book before you will show even the skeptic that he will approve of this catalog.

First, it fits into a new trend among antique lovers. Second, there is actually very little literature that treats exclusively the furniture of the Biedermeier era, and to date there has been not a single book that offers a source of type, style and price comparisons to the friend of the simple dwelling culture of those days. Thus this volume will surely fill a hole in the available literature on the subject.

The publishers are convinced of that. The authors as well, colleagues in the Stuttgart art auction house of Dr. Nagel, were on the job in the summer of 1985 when the publishers came to them with the suggestion to compile a suitable "Antique Catalog." Through their daily work with antiques, inculding those of the first half of the 19th century, they were well aware of the lack of a reference work on the subject. In the end, they needed only an impetus from outside to add the work on such a book to their daily work at the auction house.

In many "overtime hours and night shifts," there arose the book before you, the newest member of the "antique catalog" series. This book is oriented completely to reality, with a large photo section showing exclusively furniture that has been offered and auctioned in Germany in the most recent years.

An introduction shall bring the art lover and collector closer to the historical environment of the Biedermeier era. Here the contents and purpose of such a book complete each other ideally, for furniture, as an expression of the living culture of an epoch, is also a mirror of the times that are concerned here, with the beginning of a widespread historical change, a solidification of spirit and social structure that still affect our present-day life.

In this respect, Biedermeier is presented as a typically German style. For collecting as such, plus collecting of Biedermeier furniture in particular, tips and encouragement are offered, so that this volume will smooth the way for the beginner in the field of Biedermeier, a field that, as will become clear as one reads, is not always smooth. But the price guide should be understood only as a guideline, for the value to the true devotee must be left out of it.

Surely a reader will encounter misunderstanding when, in the course of purchasing negotiations, he tries to have the price of an especially well-proportioned secretary desk, that fits perfectly into the buyer's wall space, lowered purely on the basis of a similar piece shown here. Direct comparisons are only possible to a degree, and thus the cited values should only be starting points, though they are well suited to protect one from real mistakes and fully exaggerated expectations in terms of sale prices.

To keep the text realistic in this area as well, the authors were able to acquire the assistance, for the "Maintaining value through restoration and care" and "Furniture Designs" sections, of the Augsburg restorer Uwe Dobler, who has made a name for himself through his numerous accomplishments, particularly the work that he has carried out for great museums. The publishers and authors would like here to express their thanks to him for the assistance and the profound knowledge that he has contributed to this book.

In the catalog section, only such furniture will be considered as has attained a firm value in the most recent years, not excepting invaluable individual pieces. On the basis of this fact, plus the fact that experts express themslves on every area of the subject, the reader whether professional or amateur‾will hold in his hand a work that, clearly understood and properly used, can offer unique assistance to everyone who cares about furniture and Biedermeier.

Goethe's room in Tiefurt Castle, with Biedermeier furniture.

Tiefurt Castle, roll-top desk of Johann Wilhelm Kronrath, Weimar, circa 1805.

The Biedermeier Era: 1815-1850

"Biedermeier" was the time between the Wars of Liberation in 1815 and the "arch-conservatism" of 1848. Today one often one-sidedly views this era as having a spirit typified by loyalty, contemplative tranquility and narrow-minded morality. In this era the Grimm brothers collected their "Children's and Household Tales", the Frankfurt doctor Heinrich Hoffmann published his "Slovenly Peter" with didactic intent, and the painter-poet Josef Viktor von Scheffel published, in the typically petit-bourgeois "Flying Leaves" weekly, poems with such titles as "Biedermann's Pleasant Evening" and "Bummelmaier's Lament."

The names of "Biedermann" and "Bummelmeier" were combined by Ludwig Eichrodt into his pseudonym "Gottlieb Biedermaier." under which he, along with his friend, Dr. Adolf Kussmaul, the poems of the naive village schoolmaster Samuel Friedrich Sauter, in which they discovered the culmination of "comfortable Biederness". "Biedermaier" was still written with "ai" then. Only in 1869 did Eichrodt write "Biedermeier's Love for Songs", thus helping the currently used spelling to prevail.

Biedermeier as an Artistic and Cultural Concept

In this firm the concept was taken up by the following generation and linked with the scorn that one often applies in judging the old and traditional. In retrospect, one saw in Mr. "Biedermeier" only the refugee, satisfied with the small pleasures of a simple life, who had withdrawn into his four walls and praised the Creator of potatoes with Sauter's "Potato Song". This is surely not fair to the reality of life in the period from 1815 to 1848.

As a term of art history, "Biedermeier" found acceptance only around 1900, when it was recognized that artistic creation in the first half of the past century showed qualitative characteristics that differenti-ated it clearly from Empire and the subsequent Historicism. The view of Biedermeier in art history cannot, in the light of modern research, be limited to the period from 1815 to 1848. The roots of the Biedermeier style are found at the end of the 18th century. The development of a proto-Biedermeier was already taking place in the first decade of the 19th century, parallel with aristocratically elegant Empire style.

The book at hand concerns one segment of the art-historical Biedermeier, but insight into the living conditions and the political and cultural spirit of the times affords a better understanding of the era.

After all, one sees in Biedermeier furniture a document of a private philosophy of life that placed great value on the comforts of home. What moved the Biedermann to this step backward into idyllic domesticity?

Political Restoration and Withdrawal into Privacy

At the Congress of Vienna, the chance to form a unified German state was thrown away. With the German Confederation, small German states came back to life, were sorted out anew and in some cases much enlarged. Influenced by the French Revolution's spirit of freedom and under the impression of national euphoria after the victorious Wars of Liberation, a new self-awareness grew among the citizenry, only to be bitterly disappointed by the Congress of Vienna.

The July Revolution of 1830 in France also had a lasting effect on the bourgeois self-awareness in Germany. Repressed by the Carlsbad Decrees, which let loose the persecution of demagogues and forbade fraternities, political activity was possible only to a very limited extent. For instance, critical remarks in a newspaper read by the censors could result in years of imprisonment for the author. Thus the citizen drew back into private life as a well-behaved "Biedermann" and contented himself with the limited happiness of his nearest environment.

Living Conditions at the Beginning of the 19th Century

The urban citizenry was very insignificant in terms of the entire population, for in 1816 some 90% of the population still lived in the country, usually in the simplest conditions. To be sure, there were very major regional differences, influenced not only by the political situation, but also by climate and terrain.

Traveling on a mail coach was very much harder than traveling today, what with stops to change horses and at numerous toll stations. Many roads were so bad that broken wheels and axles, or capsized coaches, were no rarity. Only rich people could afford to travel in their own coaches. The "ordinary mail" coaches were simple and uncomfortable, and their fares were rather high; the journey from Kassel to Frankfurt, for example, cost 6 to 7 Taler. The express post coaches covered 400 km in two or three days. And there was no uniform system of coinage or weights and measures in Germany.

All of this made trade and the exchange of goods and ideas difficult.

The cities usually had no streetlights, and only a few streets were paved with cobblestones. Only in 1824 were the first sidewalks, called by the French term "trottoire," built in Berlin. The gutters often overflowed when it rained. The hygienic conditions in the cities, as in the country, were often catastrophic and improved only slowly. The cholera epidemic of 1830-31, which spread from Asia through Russia into all of Europe, took 1426 lives in Berlin alone.

In the Biedermeier era most cities were still surrounded by medieval city walls, fortifications and moats. The gates were closed at night, and entry and exit were watched. Inside the walls, the streets and alleys were often narrow and crooked. In the newly-built residence cities of the 17th and 18th centuries there were usually just gardens and fields inside the walls. Gardens and summerhouses, though, were often found outside the city fortifications.

The isolation of the individual cities, along with the social conditions, combined with the political repression to form the three essential factors of the Biedermeier life style of the citizenry, which grew slowly after the Wars of Liberation. The simplicity of that life style also applied to the furniture in the houses.

Progress After the Founding of the German Customs Union

Technical innovations and industrial development made the rising bourgeoisie's desire for a free market more and more urgent. Thus on January 1, 1834 the German Customs Union was formed, composed of eighteen states which no longer had to pay duties to each other. Thanks to the resulting simplification in moving trade goods, the business world could develop more freely, especially the manufacturers and factories.

Travel also became simpler, what with a developing road and rail transport system. A few figures will make the industrial development and emerging economic dynamics clear: In 1830 there were 245 steam engines in use in Prussia, in 1837 there were already 419. The number of workers also grew steadily. At the beginning of the thirties there were 450,000; in the revolution year of 1848 already a million.

The Bourgeois Homeowner

The middle-class city dweller of the Biedermeier era was a homeowner. Houses, some of considerable size, contained whole families. A comfortable dwelling included and reception or living room, the parlor, the dining room, often a workroom for the master of the house, bedrooms, nurseries, kitchen and servants' quarters.

Baths and water pipes were found very rarely in these houses. As in the 18th century, one bathed in a wooden, zinc or copper tub. It was customary for a bathhouse to lend out a tub and deliver hot water to

Goethe's garden house in the park on the Ilm.

the house with it. The walls in the house were usually whitewashed; wallpaper was found only in wealthy households. Wallpaper borders were also customary. The floors were made of boards as a rule, with parquet floors limited to castles and well-to-do households. Carpets were expensive luxury goods. Heating was usually done by burning wood in iron or tile stoves. Heat-holding double windows were still unknown except in a few castles.

A literarily clear, typically bourgeois ideal life style was described by Adalbert Stifter in a study dated April 25, 1834: "Two old desires of my heart rise up. I would like a dwelling of two big rooms, with well-built floors on which no dust settles. Soft green or pearl-gray walls, on them new objects (the term of the times for furniture), noble, massive, antiquely simple, sharp-angled and gleaming; gray silk window-curtains like gently cut glass, stretched in small folds and to be pulled from the sides to the center."

For light one still had to make do with oil lamps or tallow lights. Wax candles were very expensive and were used only by the nobility, the churches and well-to do families. Starting a fire was still laborious and time-consuming in the thirties; only in 1832 did matches begin to be manufactured in Germany.

The Bourgeois Family's Everyday Life

The garden was also a part of Biedermeier living, either at the town house or outside the gates, where well-to-do citizens also had summerhouses built. The raising, tending and collecting of plants often became a passion. Color and variety, a tendency toward overcrowding with arbors, shrubs and statues, a preference for small and playful things typified the Biedermeier garden.

As a rule, the housewife did her own cooking. Only well-to-do families ate meat dishes for dinner. With good food, they drank beer or wine, depending on the region. In their efforts to be as self-sufficient as possible, produce their own goods and buy nothing from foreign countries, it was very customary that wine was produced even in areas with unfavorable weather, until the end of the toll barriers and the advance of traffic and commerce caused such self-sufficiency to decrease gradually.

A Change Begins to Develop

Although only 25% of the people were literate around 1800, and only 30% by 1830, the level of education improved continually. The structure of the school system and the creation of the teacher class can be seen as one of the great cultural achievements of the Biedermeier era. Before that the teachers were often artisans, soldiers or university dropouts who passed on to their students only the most needed reading, writing and arithmetic.

Only now, along with the traditional elite schools in the cities, did a regulated school system arise, and the educational level of the common people improved.

With this growing level of culture there came the production of reading material: newspapers, magazines and books. Machines to make paper were introduced in Germany in 1820 and fast presses in 1832., so that German book production rose from 4375 new books in 1821 to some 7000 in 1830 and 11,000 in 1840. Along with literary works, there were also instructive publications turned out in low-cost mass production.

Finally, travel on road and rail became easier with the increasingly developed transit network. Ideas and information could be exchanged beyond local boundaries, and horizons expanded.

In the long run, the conservative powers of the Metternich era could not change this. The human and spiritual potential that had developed in Biedermeier life between 1815 and 1848 was so great that the course of history could not be held back; the March Revolution of 1848 was about to take place.

The Furniture Style

Origin, Creation, Features

In the development of the Biedermeier style, as in all the style-oriented developments of the centuries, it should be kept in mind that the new is unthinkable without what has gone before, whether in the adoption and further development of what was already at hand, or the resulting rejection of the old, which is always linked with the longing for a new outlook on life and new possibilities of artistic expression. The Biedermeier, like the Empire, is a Classic style that drew its inspirations from the antique.

Rediscovering the Antique

The Louis XVI style developing in France as well, with its striving for cubic completeness and its variety of antique-style decor elements, included both the traditional element and the reaction to the Rococo playfulness that relaxed the complete form with its asymmetrical, naturalistic ornamentation. This reaction is, on the one hand, an expression of longing for more living comfort and thus more privacy, away from the ceremony of court life, and on the other, of the artistic rediscovery of antique forms as a result of the excavation of Herculaneum (1738) and Pompeii (1755). It was French architects who first took up this new influx and adapted it to the spirit of the times, to be summoned to set new styles at the German residences in the years after 1765.

But it was also Johann Joachim Winkelmann (1717-1768), the German scholar of antiquity, whose writings brought an influence, not to be overlooked, on the German development of clear architectural forms in connection with ornamentation in antique style. But as willingly as architecture accepted the new style, the more hesitantly did furniture making in Germany take on this new challenge.

British Models · Late Rococo

Above all, it was Britain whose models were to characterize the balanced "Queue Style", for a development toward classic furniture style had already taken place there in the 18th century. The striving for more fidelity to the material and functionality of furniture in the sense of a new practicality and comfort was represented there from 1765 on, particularly by the Scottish architect Robert Adam (1728-1792).

But the British furniture designer George Hepplewhite (+ 1786), in his design manual "The Cabinet-Maker's and Upholsterer's Guide", as well as Thomas Sheraton (1751-1806) in "The Cabinet Maker's and Upholsterer's Drawing Book", represented the new trend in the eighties and nineties with practically conceived furniture designs, most of which were very elegant.

Mobility was desired, various new types of furniture such as worktables, etageres or toilet cabinets with complex interior layouts now found a firm place in modern living concepts.

The Queue Style or Louis XVI Style essentially spread east of the Rhine and found its characteristic forms and elements of style only after 1780. These are symmetrical architectural structure with a striving for cubic completion, conical square or round legs that stressed the lightness of the furniture, and the prismatic forms of the body with more sparing antique decor that was now used for deliberate effects, [p. 16] partly as marquetry or intarsia, partly in the use of bronze fittings.

"Good Taste" Prevails

The Queue Style, borne by this new basic understanding of furniture building toward the end of the 18th century, and Britain with its documented influence on this epoch of style and the subsequent Empire, were to lead to three defining influences in both cause and effect on the development of the Biedermeier style.

On the Continent, more and more publications with prints of patterns appeared; the most important and influential was probably the "Journal des Luxus und der Moden", published in Weimar since 1785. They influenced the furniture makers in the various German regions to varying degrees.

In the 1790s there developed, especially in Brandenburg, Saxony and Thuringia, a proto-Biedermeier style. One example is the furnishing of Paretz Castle near Berlin, in addition to many pieces of furniture in Weimar. In illustrations, the Weimar high society of the nineties sits on such furniture.

At the same time, and continuing into the 1830s in bourgeois circles, Louis XVI furniture in almost pure form, and sometimes dated, was being made, especially of oak and cherry. In the first two decades of the 19th century, many pieces of Franconian and Munich Biedermeier furniture are known to have been owned by the Wittelsbachs, the Bavarian royal family.

After 1810 most of the earlier profiles, stripes and steps disappeared. Paw feet are usually limited to the time between 1805 and 1820. Between 1815 and 1835 rectangular block feet were common, paralleled by four-sided tapered feet, and as of 1820 curving and saber-like feet became more widespread. The artistic elements were those of Classicism, but they had to subordinate themselves to the flat surfaces, and bronze was often replaced by gilded wood. Thus three-dimensional masses were used on a base of sawdust and other "mixed materials". Horns of plenty, dolphins and swans appeared on the arms of sofas or on table frames.

Paw feet were also still used for chests and table legs. But a common change is seen in all of them; they appear less naturalistic, but rather stylized and are also formed more tenderly. Thus they represent the adaptation that was already completed in Viennese Empire style.

Bronze hardware did not appear to decorate surfaces, as in Empire style, but was only used individually and purposefully as handles or lock shields. Most of the time pressed sheet brass was preferred. Some of these fittings were imported from Britain, but they were also manufactured in the German lands. Often the hardware is completely omitted, shield- and diamond-shaped lock shields made of ebonized wood or bone were used in their place. Thereby the chosen structure of the varnished wood was supposed to have a greater effect.

The pierced backs of chairs, as already in the Queue Style, offered many decorative possibilities. The lyre should be mentioned, for it enjoyed great popularity. It served as a decorative ornament, was included in designs of table supports and sides, and dominated whole forms of furniture, though often stylized and only to be imagined.

Regional Differences

In the southern lands, cherry and walnut furniture was most popular, In Vienna and North Germany, mahogany furniture, and ib central and eastern Germany ash and birch as well as mahogany. In addition, elm, pear, apple, poplar and other woods were used. Maple was used primarily for inlays. These, though, were not small marquetry surfaces, but rather economical and cautious accentuation with folding stars, tendrils, flowers, umbrella or sea-shell motifs. Partial blackening of the maple by burning in hot sand became rarer. Frame stripes and ribbon inlays never unified the entire form, but contoured the individual cubes.

Only in the formation of something like a secretary interior does one see and sense the pressure and the creative demands of marquetry. Different-colored woods, plays of perspective, walls, diamond and cube designs and small architectonic details indicate this,

Bureau, Vienna, circa 1810.

but are not visible when the writing panel is closed. Also deserving of note in this respect are the black-lead paintings, transfers and various markings that were made on the wood.

Making frame-filling designs visible was avoided when possible, so as not to influence the flat surfaces. If this turned up, it was weakened by the veneer that covered everything uniformly and rose up longitudinally. The veneer was applied broadside and tilted around a central axis, thus intensifying the flatness. Through this even "outer skin", various formations such as friezes, insets in the shape of arcs, diamonds or rectangles fit in with the surface effects. Whole pieces of furniture, especially small ones, were built up to form a ball.

Technical Innovation

In technical terms there were many innovations in tools and machines, such as pad saws, improved planes, sawing, boring, slitting and veneer-cutting machines. And yet until the middle of the century⁻with regional differences⁻a clinging to traditional manufacturing techniques prevailed.

It must be pointed out that [p. 18] veneered furniture was the exception not only in well-to-do bourgeois households, but even among the nobility. Except at the royal courts there was far more softwood furniture as well as pieces made of oak or massive cherry or walnut. The general rarity of veneered furniture is shown by many inventories.

Developments and Reception

Fruit-tree woods became more and more popular. It was primarily the wood of wild-growing trees that was used, not those planted in orchards. The vertical grain of the veneer defines the furniture as a standing total form. In high-value furniture the veneer grain is usually symmetrical on an axis.

Increasing stocks of ready-made furniture required a standardization of their appearance. Because of the beauty of the veneer pattern, hardware, as noted above, was usually omitted altogether. In the south in particular, pressed sheet brass fittings in very many variations of form were used instead of handmade ones.

The time of hierarchically grouped, high-class sets of furniture was past; small groups of furniture appeared. The seats of chairs were stuffed with sea grass, animal hair or straw above a base of woven belts. Late in the Biedermeier era the first iron springs appeared.

Anti-classic Tendencies and Free Formation in Late Biedermeier

Until 1830 the Biedermeier furniture can be regarded as a styling trend based on Classicism. From 1830 on, and strongly after 1835, a relaxing of forms began, corners became rounded, additional profiles and carvings were added. Legs, rungs and fillings had more curves, and turned pieces became more common. The basic form was often modernized in the sense of a no longer exclusive one-sided view. Rounded and additionally ribbed angles of the piece led the eye to the sides and blended into them. The same effect was gained with decorative profiles including three sides, or those with waves and bulges, friezes penetrating and articulating the surfaces. Along with a double scroll used as a closing, this created a kind of dissolution of the clear outline of earlier furniture.

Richly flowing in forms progressing to silhouettes are the base plates, feet, legs, backs, arms, rungs and surfaces. The central columns of tables were made stronger after 1830 and thus often appear un-sharp. Cornice curves were often used after 1835 in profiles, top rails and drawer fronts. The furniture thus acquired a profile again and became easier to conceive from a side view.

Another important characteristic of the late form is the sometimes overstated progressive enrichment of various ornamental forms.

Flower, tendril and leaf decor encompassing all three visible sides, as well as sometimes historical marquetry became popular. Plastically shaped or relief decorations appeared more and more often after 1845. Horns of plenty, swans, eagles, fan shapes and leaves may dominate whole parts of benches and other seat furniture.

Temporal Parallels: Late Empire and Biedermeier

Until 1840 there was a parallel development of furnishings in late Empire style for elegant and public rooms. Neo-gothic forms appeared more frequently in the late days of Biedermeier for groups of furniture and in seat backs. The same applies as of about 1840 for elements of Historicism. The more and more frequent expositions, fairs and catalogs did much to set the styles.

Mirrored etagere from Bembe, Mainz, circa 1836.

Wilhelm Kimbel of Mainz and *Johann Geyer* of Innsbruck, and their workshops, may be noted here as two typically outstanding personalities in the design and building of furniture in the late Biedermeier style. Their furniture typifies the use of earlier forms and inclusion of previous elements of style.

Obsolescence and Rediscovery of Biedermeier Style

Only Historicism and the industrialization that was linked with it, which set in around the middle of the 19th century in their all-encompassing consequence, conjured up the end of the Biedermeier style. Still in all, *Michael Thonet* (1796-1871) of Boppard on the Rhine had already begun to develop series production of his bent-wood furniture with interchangeable parts. Only after his move to Vienna in 1842, though, did he attain a breakthrough and international renown.

Around 1895, after the Biedermeier style had been laughed at and satirized for half a century, were the first signs of rehabilitation of the Biedermeier era and its style seen. In 1896 the Austrian Museum of Art and Industry in Vienna set up a noteworthy exposition concerning the Congress of Vienna. Observations of the history of art ensued, in which Biedermeier often appeared along with Empire as its derivative. But the independence of this style was recognized more and more. In this respect, its furniture was also reevaluated correspondingly.

This tendency, just as Art Nouveau arose from the reaction to the pluralism of style and variety of form that typified Historicism, utilized Empire and Biedermeier equally in looking back at "antique virtues". At the expositions, furnishings of entire rooms in Biedermeier style were now shown. On the one hand, this involved furniture that was copied faithfully from historical models, on the other, forms were imitated in modified ways. For functionality and fidelity to material, both typical qualities of Biedermeier, were recognized and valued again around 1900.

Furniture Types

At the time of the Congress of Vienna, the public architectural style, as before, was that of early Classicism. The modest bourgeois house and the rented house in which various "parties" lived under one roof could not escape from this style. Here too, a reduction to a realistic form of design with balanced proportions can be seen. Thus the architecture reflected the typical inward trend of Biedermeier.

Interiors of the time are known to us from oil and water-color paintings, and especially from the engravings that were so universally popular in those days. As their focal point, they often show the ideal patriarchal family amid reduced but still love-blessed circumstances, or a social occasion with music, cards or reading. It is not the high-class, elegant salon that is the site of daily get-togethers; it is the living room that, with its bright layout, promotes a pleasant form of life and living culture as its basic unity. A symmetrical arrangement of furniture is only found where there is enough room for it.

The living quarters were painted in light colors or whitewashed, for covering the walls in paper was reserved only for the well-to-do upper bourgeois. An ornamental frieze set off the wall surfaces from the ceiling, which was often decorated with a stucco rosette. From the center of the ceiling there hung decorations made of wood or other materials. The floor consisted of planed planks or boards; seldom was it parqueted.

The furniture suited the available space in terms of size and shape, just as it suited the human proportions. A general desire for harmony between man and his world inspired furniture to be made in those days that reflected this symbiotic relationship; furniture that expressed simplicity and comfort˗which is why they are still desired furnishings today.

Bureaus and Writing Desks

As already in the 18th century, *bureaus* enjoyed great popularity. Clothes and linens were stored in them. The *chiffonier* or pillar bureau, although known already in the 18th century, developed into a typical item of the time. These bureau types that extended upward often had their accepted place on a wall between two windows. *Stacked showcases* formed popular combinations of the two noted types of furniture.

In addition to these common pieces, writing bureaus, bureau-secretaries with cylinders or angled writing panels, writing tables with side drawers, often usable on both sides, or those with a boxy upper part that moved back, enjoyed much popularity.

An important place was taken by the *writing cabinet* in the living room. It usually had a smooth front. The traditional superstructure has two or three drawers in its lower reaches, and over them the big folding writing panel, and at the upper end of the body a worked-in top drawer. Above the closing plate, an architectonically formed top usually arises in northern and central Germany. The inner arrangements, hidden behind the writing panel, often were richly compartmented.

With their numerous drawers, letter spaces and pigeonholes, as well as the highly valued secret compartments, they gave the artisan all kinds of possibilities for exhibiting his ability and creative gifts. The man of the house, as user of this furniture, treasured these manifold characteristics. They offered him space for documents, letters or daybooks as well as his personal collections, which meant a lot to the well-to-do bourgeois.

The *writing furniture* for the ladies was more delicate. Most of them could stand free in a room and thus they are veneered on all sides. [p. 21] They too are often fitted with lavish facilities and are admirably suited for preserving typically feminine accessories: albums of poetry, mementos of social and family occasions, as well as letters.

Cupboards, Cases and Chests

The *cupboard,* traditional storage place for clothing and linens, could also maintain its popularity during the Biedermeier era. As a rule it stood in a front room or in the hall. The so-called *Blender* had variants. Linen cupboards, their fronts divided like those of a writing bureau, were equipped with all the appropriate details. Only when one opened the full-width doors could they be recognized as linen cupboards.

The *showcase* also stood in a preferred place in the salon or living room. It served to contain those romantic-sentimental treasures like souvenir plates, club or friendship mugs, miniatures, bouquets in glass balls, and travel souvenirs. Often glassed on three sides and mirrored inside, they proudly showed off the treasures within. But porcelain dishes, glass or silver objects, which were only put on the table for holidays or special occasions were also kept in them in a decorative manner.

More strongly built and usually only glassed in front, yet more richly decorated and reinforced showcases served as *bookcases.* They are usually much shallower than showcases. Bookcases displayed the owner's erudition and were meant to document awareness of the world and interest in literature and art.

The desire for comfort plus optimal utilization of the available space resulted in numerous *corner stands.* Corner showcases, cupboards and half-cupboards, their fronts often bowed, rounded off the complete picture of the room and created additional storage space.

Tables

Even though family life was carried on, the desire for individual space in mutually used areas arose. These "living islands" were characterized by their specific furniture.

The *table* took on a hitherto unknown significance in this division of roles it became the unifying meeting place and focal point of the family. People gathered around it and met at it for the most varied reasons. The table was not placed in the center of the room to eat up space, but put near the wall or in a corner. It also served for family meals, but beyond that, people gathered around it for mutual reading and misic-making, handicrafts and games.

With its form usually round, it sets no directions, for it is usually equally accessible from all sides, and thus without a seating hierarchy. The surface often features a star-shaped decor of carefully chosen veneer and is bordered by a slim decorative ring. This affords comfortable seating on the basis of its height, without needlessly mistreating its users' knees.

Built-in drawers or legs at the sides, of course, affected the designs of the wider drum rims. A powerful central pillar, offering many possibilities for shaping, often supports the tabletop. It usually stands on a three- or four-footed scroll-shaped base, though suitably curved-in or angular feet also occur. In addition there were combinations of both: volute legs, saber legs, column legs or even legs in the shape of dolphins being popular.

Along with the round types there were oval and rectangular "sofa tables", sometimes with folding-down sides, which were very popular in northern and central Germany thanks to the British influence. Also [p. 22] based on British and French models were the semicircular *wall tables,* often a gate-leg and folding panel; *gaming tables* had similar designs.

Small Furniture

The *console,* along with the pillar mirror rising above it, found popularity as before as room-forming and light-enhancing elements. Much more often, bureaus were found between windows, and with mirrors above them, in Biedermeier interiors.

Work, sewing, flower, end, toilet and similar *tables* are popular because of their special functions. Elaborately decorated examples have numerous small draw-

Georg Friedrich Kersting, *The Embroiderer,* 1811, with simple Biedermeier cherrywood furniture.

ers, compartments, folding mirrors, paint pots, pincushions or writing implements. The imagination and artisans' skills of their makers are expressed most impressively in their free forms. But they also reflected the noble or bourgeois position of their Biedermeier-era housewives and the homey virtues they followed.

Etageres and *vitrines* were also popular, those open structures that likewise served as places to put all kinds of useful things, or that held the dishes and baked goods for the afternoon tea or coffee hour.

Chairs and Couches

The creation and the accepted forms of seating furniture were very manifold. The un-upholstered open backs of the *chairs* invited artistic decoration. Simple crosspieces, bowed fan ribs, shaped lyres, segments of circles, vase shapes, carved central tongues or three-dimensional dolphins were used to decorate the surface between the lower crosspiece and upper shoulder board. The front of the upholstered seat usually rested on straight or curved rectangular legs, the rear on extended ones. They generally ran conically toward each other and thus expressed a lightness that was striven for then, along with antique-style ornamentation.

A variant of the *armchair, easy chair* or *bergere* was the *wing chair.* Into it the man of the house withdrew after the burdens of the day were dealt with. Clad in his dressing gown and stocking cap, he leaned back and relaxed as he followed the latest events by reading the newspapers and magazines, finally giving in to the pleasures of smoking. Exhausted and weary from the pressure of events and pleasures, his care-laden head found comfortable support on the side "wings" of the chair back. Caricatures show this, and thus was this era characterized and satirized by succeeding generations.

The *sofa* became the characteristic seating furniture, the incorporation of all that was Biedermeier, even to the point of pushing several armchairs into the background. In its very external, "all-inclusive" form, it represents the essence of Biedermeier. As the dominant focal point of the sitting group, the sofa stood behind the table and offered two or three people a comfortable seat for pleasant and social togetherness. The armrests were often decoratively ornamented. The decor ranged from simple curves to columns, scrolls or rolls and on to very three-dimensional horns of plenty and dolphins. The sitting and leaning surfaces were upholstered and often enriched with cushions and bolsters. The costs of high-quality upholstery materials were considerable, and their colors were often very intensive. "Biedermeier fabrics" with stripes and flower patterns, on the other hand, are only an invention of the so-called Second Biedermeier era after 1900.

On the other hand, the *bench* had open backs and arms, and showed many of the same artistic decorations as the chairs. Small seating furniture such as *stools, tabourets* and *footstools* complete the ranks of the seating furniture.

Beds

The variety of Biedermeier furniture could be continued at impressive length, and thus can only be portrayed below by typical examples. The *beds,* often including a compartmented headboard, were often placed in an alcove and were closed off by a canopy or draperies. *Cradles* reflected parental pride and joy in their artistic designs.

Other Furniture

Upright and *grand pianos* give evidence of lively household music. The *"giraffe" grand piano* with its striking, extended resonating chamber ranks among the most beautiful of all instruments.

Mirrors are to be found in many forms, from simple board frames to architectonic window frames, plus the standing "psyche" mirrors that were essential to ladies as they dressed.

Lampshades and *stove screens* often bore effect-heightening paintings or were decorated with naively artistic embroidery. In addition, bobbin stands and handiwork stands were widespread as sites for the creation of lovingly made objects of homey energy.

All of these small pieces and utility items are ultimately useful things, whose presence and variety document the Biedermeier era.

Furniture Designs

Appearance

In a book on Biedermeier furniture that has the purpose of offering the collector, interested party and friend of this furniture an overview of the market situation and simultaneously standing by one as a practical advisor, even when buying such a piece, it must not lack an introduction to their construction and a description of the original, un-falsified and also restored condition of this furniture. The outer appearance, as well as the design of the furniture, is decisive for their value. The question of authenticity is not answerable without knowledge of their design and workmanship. Therefore in the text the reader shall be given a technical guide to this justified need for information.

Material and design took on considerably greater importance in furniture at the beginning of the 19th century than had generally been the case in the 18th century. It is not so much the decoration, the art of marquetry, the spatial, sometimes perspective play of the various veneer woods or the elements often adopted from architecture, such as columns, bases, capitals and right-angle joints characterize the appearance of Biedermeier furniture, but rather the large clear flat surfaces and the sober, usually right-angled body. Its only decoration is often the chosen veneer pattern, whose course runs homogeneously over drawers, flaps, doors, crosspieces and friezes, whereby the total optical impression is disturbed by as few design-caused interruptions and distractions as possible.

Of course one also encounters in Biedermeier, especially in northern Germany and Brandenburg, elements of classic architecture that have been taken over unchanged. They often have a strict, drawn, tense arched or linear effect and blend harmoniously into the external sobriety of the object. Defining details seldom occur; rather, one senses the pressure of the decorative elements to subordinate themselves to the total picture.

A further very important characteristic of style is the so-called "one-sidedness", meaning the decorative concentration on the frontal facade. It is especially noticeable in container furniture. But the chair, the bench and the sofa also have a segmented facade and do not create their full effect when viewed from the side. In many cases, in fact, the complete appearance cannot even be suspected from this perspective.

In most cases, one sees furniture from the Biedermeier era at once in an "optical total picture". The piece can be comprehended at the first glance, and the eye, so to speak, does not get lost in details. Perhaps this is the reason why the interest of the buyer-to-be who formerly had little to do with antiques is often captured by Biedermeier furniture. One often hears such reasons as, "the furniture does not dumbfound me" or "it harmonizes best with my layout, "or "I could imagine myself living with such furniture." All these arguments prove that the demands made by Biedermeier furniture on their observer and on spatial integration are not as great as those of furniture from the 17th and 18th centuries. A further reason is that the size of Biedermeier furniture is suitable for modern dwellings.

Placing Furniture in Rooms, Woodworking Techniques, Design

In the Biedermeier era furniture increasingly lost its firm, prominent place in space. For the placing of furniture, the ideal of axial symmetry originally applied, whereby for every piece of furniture a pendant was to be created in the room. Whether it was the high cost of obtaining furniture or unsuitable spatial conditions,

The salon of Princess Mathilde in the Munich Residence, Lorenzo Quaglio, 1832, with a
chiffonier from the Daniel Court Carpentry Shop, circa 1810, at left.

in any case this principle of arrangement fades more
and more into the background in favor of a freer arrangement of the room. Criteria such as livability, use-
fulness and comfort, as well as affordability, became
more and more decisive.

Under these conditions the attention of the carpenter was drawn more to the "inner life" of the furniture. At the same time, the sober outer appearance
required a high degree of precision, since unevenness
in the work could no longer, as in the 18th century, be
concealed with the help of lavish decoration. What
unevenness in design and workmanship was evened
out in earlier style epochs by refined decor now was
clear to see. Thus in the case of a folding-in, smoothly
fitting and undecorated writing panel, with a border
just millimeters wide all around, it was not possible to
put on a profile that would have hidden the uneven-

ness in this border, which one would rather have
avoided entirely. The carpenter could not touch up a
veneer pattern that continued onto all sides of the
body. This enforced precision demanded exact workmanship and a technical refinement of the furniture.

So it is no surprise that some innovations that were
reserved only for especially elaborate furniture late in
the 18th century could take hold quickly in
Biedermeier. Among them were many new features
that do not become visible at first glance and represent exclusively technical advantages, such as improved
drawer sliding, low-torsion flat elements, invisible turning technology or transition from turning to sliding
motion in cylinder furniture. This makes it understand-
able why Biedermeier furniture on the basis of its manifold technical innovations, holds an outstanding place
in the history of furniture making.

Surely it is not the design alone that proves the originality of a Biedermeier piece, and many design solutions are not pure inventions of Biedermeier times. Yet there are large numbers of techniques, connections and design details that found general application only in this style trend.

The decisive style element of Biedermeier furniture is the cube, the simple box in all forms, proportions, designs and variations.

The path to this form leads along the simple board. It is found at every position in all its possible styles and expressions, to the finest detail of the decor. The whole piece is made up of this element as worked by the artisan, and thus the board is the outstanding characteristic of the furniture. The design "transparency" lets the observer understand the artisan's creation, such as no other furniture style trend allows in a similarly clear way.

For the design of box furniture, this chiefly meant a board construction of the sides with precise swallowtail dovetailing. Often it is half covered, since the body angles often end only in veneer and the area critical to the evenness of the veneer is not, as in the 18th century, surrounded by a plinth, front or wreath profile. A higher number of dovetails than in earlier eras is typical, in order to avoid too-wide swallowtail sections and thus prevent breakage.

Yet especially dovetailed and over-veneered body angles now rank among the areas in which veneer damage often occurs, brought on by wood shrinkage. Many swallowtails "disappear" in the dovetails, the resulting height difference expels the veneer to almost the same extent, and breakage results.

But besides the simple dovetailed board side or top there is also the veneered frame with plain filling.

It occurs more rarely on the actual body, but is often used on the lowering panels of the writing cabinets or the removable writing panels of cylinder or roll-top secretaries. Here the disappearance of the plain wood is almost without significance for the veneer, but on massive sides with veneer running in the same direction it often leads to ugly cracks.

Surely the frame construction was not a cure-all for cracking in veneer. As a rule, they occur in this design only with excessively low dampness of the air in the room, which will be dealt with in the chapter on conservation (see p. 40). The technique of preventing wood breakage (veining of veneer and wood underneath running at right angles to each other), in which one makes use of the different directions of cracking, was not used on purpose in Biedermeier but, if it occurred at all, did so by chance, usually when the design resulted in it anyway.

As a rule, the veneer runs vertically on all sides that show. The sides, including those of dovetailed designs, were laid out vertically, the same as the veneer, and only rarely does it occur in bureaus that the veneer on the sides is horizontal, and almost not at all for the wood underneath. The top, as a rule, runs lengthwise in board construction. Here with veneer grains running at right angles there was a blocking-off effect.

Yet with large cracks in the wood underneath, despite the dovetailed corner design, it can result in a strong bulging of the panels, which in this case can be ascribed to the blocking. For the most part, this blocking takes place in the drawers of bureaus and writing cabinets. Here the combined vertical veneer pattern is on crosswise drawer fronts, usually with half-concealed dovetailing.

Often one can see a bulging of these front pieces as a very strong breaking effect In rare cases it happens that, caused by a wrong choice of the wood underneath, a concave bulge occurs. Even then the rule of thumb for veneered drawer fronts applies: Angle to the inside, meaning that the outside of the tree wood of the front board should form its inside.

A further variation of the blocking of veneered surfaces is formed by the veneer sheets of round tables. Here a star-like blocking effect was formed by segments of a circle arranged around a central point or field. This circular arrangement creates an even standing of the tabletop, as long as the choice of the basic wood is suitable. Often these tabletops, like most massive surfaces, were additionally safeguarded, simply or doubly, against breakage with inserted so-called standing or lying edge ridges. Sometimes just a glued-on traverse frieze was used, continuing to the edges and taking over the job of maintaining this security at an angle to that of the wood underneath.

A blocking on both sides, such as has become generally widespread since the beginning of the 20th century through the modern way of building surfaces, was very rare at the beginning of the 19th century, and used exclusively as a means of design. This veneering of the basic wood on both sides, which afforded a very high degree of standing stability when applied correctly, was usually used then only when both optical and esthetic requirements were to be met. Thus one finds two-sided veneering only on furniture components that are seen on both sides, such as writing panels, tabernacle and small chest doors, folding lids and folding-up gaming-table panels, in interior features of writing desks, changing tables, sewing tables or secretaries.

An achievement of the Biedermeier era that goes back to French models of the 18th century are the rails used on oval or round tables. They consist of a wooden ring composed of several layers of circle segments, are set back under the tabletop, and likewise secure the top against cracking. This multi-layered construction is static to the greatest degree and, in an impressive manner, blends an effective optical blind with fine woodworking technique.

Besides the veneered surfaces of the sides that showed, the Biedermeier carpenter also made use of another very high-quality design, which blended functionality, stability and mechanics in the most splendid way. Here the edge ridges may be named first of all. These, as already noted, consist of a wooden frieze inserted in swallowtail manner in one to two thirds of the thickness of the wood. In addition to securing the surface against splitting, it provides a good union of surfaces, which affords many design possibilities. These include guide rails for horizontal movement, principally the rails of drawers. These are set into the sides, usually refined as regular running rails with a traverse frieze at the front, visibly dividing the front between the drawers.

Someties this frame is completed by a rear traverse which is similarly dovetailed in back. Thus it becomes a stabilizing and functional refinement of the whole design, such as appeared mainly in the growing technical approach to furniture design in the early 19th century and is often to be found in precise workmanship in Biedermeier furniture.

In massive form the ridge often appears also as a guide in the sliding-out writing panels of the cylinder and roll-top secretaries, as well as the tablet slides of the secretary desks and richly appointed writing cabinets.

Likewise it often serves to anchor and guide drawers (in the case of installation or removal) of the multiunit built-in chests which, covered by the closed writing panel, are part of the inner fittings of writing cabinets.

In addition, the earlier post construction was refined. While the corner post, a carrying post foot on which the whole body design was suspended, often was still recognizable as such in the 18th century, in the 19th it drew back more and more from the vertical contour and gave way almost exclusively to surfaces in Biedermeier. Thus it is no longer recognizable as a supporting design element. This required the most extreme precision of the design for the desired flatness of the sides that showed, such as the side frames or the board surfaces between them. In the same way, traverse and plinth friezes, rails, intermediate drawer fronts, writing flaps and doors also had to fit. As a component of the plane surface, the post had no decorative significance any more and chiefly served the technical requirement for high-quality designs. As a high point of this building style, the post, no longer raised in space, reappears through an appropriately formed veneer picture.

The mortise too‾in comparison to the ridge a leading groove extending at right angles‾gained more and more importance. While in the earlier frame construction at most the filling was so fitted, now one often finds the mortised rear wall slid in from the bottom, drawer bottoms fitted in the same way, and bottom panels of bureaus and small pieces slid in from the back.

Cubic Designs and Decor Elements

Through the aforementioned stylistic reduction of the decoration on the board, the doubling of board friezes, the lengthwise gluing of the board and thus the simple flat massive gluing flourished as never before. It was doubled or glued in every imaginable way, and the cube grew into smaller cubes in space.

Plinth feet were doubled, taking more space, but kept strictly in the framework of the furniture and often served as bases for full or half columns, pilasters or lisenes, which in turn were combined stylistically only from individual pieces of board. The simple encircling socket profile is a glued-on board, often veneered crosswise to create a vertical effect, but simple and only a double. The front frame construction sticks strictly to the laws of surfaces, is stepped increasingly or decreasingly, and flat.

Capitals in the form of quadrants appear to seize space as little as completing upper profiles, which are often formed from only a simple surrounding and projecting board.

The visible side is formed horizontally by steps, strict cornice closings and projecting head fields, seldom by vertical projecting breaks in the strict course of the flat surface, such as occur as stylistic remains of an earlier flowing display side in very early Biedermeier bureaus.

Decorative table, Vienna, circa 1805.

The surface decoration is limited to simple rectangle or polygon fields, diamonds, rhombuses and circle segments¯again a decor that is to be reduced to the simple board.

In elaborately formed pieces the crowning of the secretaries and writing cabinets shows numerous elements of classic architecture. Here a simple step design was used. The post became a stylized obelisk, the construction is squared, cubed, refined with friezes and borders; everything is glued on smoothly.

The classical frieze, often borne by columns, seldom correctly profiled, closes off the vertical formation, laid dully on column tops and sidewalls and without extending into the space. As a closing one finds the flat triangular gable from antique days, again surmounted by the setback flat board box, the simple projecting top plate or the severe step gable.

Often such formations are found in Berlin furniture. In addition, especially in northern Germany and Thuringia, the simple balustrade was popular as a border. All these elements appear without technical functions, glued together dully without movement, and thus are visible optically again as a combination of the carved board.

If optical movement appears now against this cubic formation, it is always tensed, corved and usually gained from the flat surface. The movement no longer has effect out of the contour of the furniture, but remains limited to its outline.

The resulting forms are often new. The chair legs are carved, conically arranged, the back is inclined, everything has come about as if under power. Even the emphasized middle of a chair-back was apparently formed under pressure. Much has developed out of beginnings in the 1790s.

The withdrawal of form is likewise recognizable in the concavely drawn-in base of a console table, as in the elliptical or drum-shaped tabernacle crowns of some north German and Brandenburg writing cabinets. It can be perceived on the curved-in staves that accompany the central column of a round table just as in the "horn-of-plenty"-shaped arm of a sofa.

The round cupola, the spherical body of the so-called globe tables, the drum shape or ellipse, the concave entrance of sides that show or the curved glass, the lyre feet of sewing tables and simple curved foot designs, all have something in common: They are shapes sawed out of the board, without filling the space in an additional direction. Every movement runs in an arch to a previously set fixed point without extensions, decorations and essential changes of direction. Even the round body is composed of boards that are fitted exactly, often running vertically or combined as a segmented ring, and then sawn and polished.

In conclusion is can be said that Biedermeier furniture is made extremely two-dimensional compared to the three-dimensionality common to much Rococo furniture.

Mechanical Developments; metal fittings

Along with the innovations in wood construction methods in the Biedermeier era, more and more new technical methods also appeared. Above all, these include metal fittings that, cut especially to suit the requirements of the surfaces, were refined steadily. There were reasons why the so-called pivot band became more and more important. Ideal on account of its pivoting point in the surface and its exclusive fastening in the top wood or crosspiece of the element to be hinged, it completely meets the requirements and laws of the surface. With this "invisible" hardware it was possible to integrate precisely fitting moving parts into the closed flat surface.

These fittings were used even for the swinging movement of a folding card table. Here the so-called gaming-table hinge for pieces that fold one each other also appeared; the turning point lies on the intended axis of symmetry of the two panels, thus right in the butt-joint of the folded table. Attached over the upper front and otherwise largely invisible for the playing surface, it offers a satisfactory solution, rooted in the 18th century.

The lock was also moved into the flat surface, no longer raised above it, but coming out from inside, or set or cut into the wood.

Thus technology disappeared more and more from the visible realm. The escutcheon of a set-in lock on a writing panel forms only a fine technical component of the surface. As a set-in lock, it disappears optically almost completely.

Along with the various lock techniques, a precise description of which would explode from the limits of this book, the means of transmission used in transferring movement should also be noted. In the form of turning and pushing rods, they were used in the motion technology of the cylinder secretaries, convertible furniture, and sometimes in the hidden mecha-

nisms of writing desks. They serve to transmit power, to change pushing to turning motion, of levering and bridging of closing mechanisms.

Even though only particularly finely made furniture was fitted with such refinements, we can still speak of a high point for these techniques in the furniture construction of the Biedermeier era. Without the cooperation of a skillful metalworker or the adaptation of hardware available from catalogs, the carpenter could scarcely meet the competition any more.

While in the past the carpenter's ability was seen mainly in the techniques that created the outer appearance of the furniture, its expressiveness, now he worked his way into the object. Thus besides the appearance and the artistic formation of the furniture, the technical perfection too was often decisive in the success of an artisan in the first half of the 19th century.

More and more, Biedermeier furniture was no longer built to the customer's order, but made for a dealer's stock. Thanks to certain uniformity, later additional purchases were possible, for veneered furniture or the purchase of a complete set would often have been beyond the financial power of most bourgeois.

Pair of bureaus, Vienna, circa 1810.

Furniture Areas and Centers

As in the 18th century, the decisive artistic impulses came mainly from the courts and residences. Their influence thus had a style-forming effect on furniture as well, affecting certain guilds and areas. The courtly model, the firmly outlined guild regulations and customs borders caused furniture to be created in those times, and our analysis of its styles can point more or less exactly to its area of origin.

At the beginning of the Biedermeier era these factors lost their validity only slowly. In the ensuing industrialization of Historicism, the traces of furniture's origins disappeared more and more. Thus it is often difficult, especially for later Biedermeier furniture, to spot local characteristics.

The often simple, reduced furniture style, countless carpenters' designs and collections of drawings, plus the travels of furniture artisans, particularly the journeymen, affected the moving and mixing of many style elements. The attributing to certain masters, areas and centers, like that of art objects in general, may be undertaken only with foresight and caution for home furnishings of that era.

Vienna, Austria, Bohemia and Hungary

The Austro-Hungarian monarchy with its metropolis of Vienna, residence of the German Emperor until 1806, political capital of Europe during the Congress of Vienna, was also a center and focal point of the Biedermeier era in a social sense. From there, where a materially secure and prosperous bourgeoisie played a culture-supporting role along with the nobility and church, the most fruitful inspirations spread out.

Based in the finally successful rejection of French predominance, Vienna was in many ways a spiritual and artistic center, strong enough to blend the most varied impulses into its own synthesis. Already in the production of Empire-style furniture, the Vienna furniture builders had found their definitive expression. Their more cherished and fantasy-filled designs differed clearly from those of French taste and the latter's German derivatives. Their furniture is lighter and designed for livability, elegance and private life.

Angled-off corners with columns and an airy lower structure take away the strict, space-seizing effect of the cube. New furniture forms arose from the oval or the lyre, whether developed as secretaries or applied as design elements. Sphinxes, lions, and griffins (frozen into heraldic symbols) were replaced by swans, caryatids and antique-like figural elements. These were often not cast in bronze but carved in wood, and usually covered in gold leaf. This was not done just for esthetic reasons, though, but also for economy, since fire-gilded bronzes were several times more expensive. The bronze hardware used depicted horns of plenty, vases, garlands and scenes from Greek mythology, usually applied economically.

In Vienna veneered mahogany was usually worked, sometimes livened up by added ornamental bands or painted marquetry. In the country, cherry and walnut prevailed as veneering woods. Pine dominated as the covered wood.

Proceeding from this secure native comprehension of form, the production of Viennese Biedermeier furniture can be seen more than elsewhere in its relationship to and partial transition from "Empire style", and it shows itself in especially striking, artistically mature products of high quality. The preference for unconventional, spirited shapes can be seen in the lyre secretaries known since the Empire era. Here a detail used until then as a decorative element defines the entire outline of a piece of furniture.

A further example is the scroll. It appears on chiffoniers, bureaus and night tables as a form-determining body, just as on the arms of sofas or the feet of tables, where the bottom, in roll form, often serves as a stand.

Just as surely is the symbiotic play of various juxtaposed and interpenetrating geometrical forms mastered: circle, oval, cylinder, rectangle and trapezoid appear in harmony with columns, shafts, curved elements and integrated flat surfaces. The tendency toward curved surfaces finds its zenith in the masterful creation of hemispherical sewing stands and completely spherical globe tables.

Although the British cabinetmaker George Remmington obtained a patent for similar writing desks as early as 1806, these jewels of Biedermeier furniture art attained their true perfection in the hands of the Vienna ebonists, and in their artistic and technical precision they rank among the most beautiful and valuable creations that we know from that era.

To what a high degree the Viennese, as well as the Bohemian and Hungarian Biedermeier furniture is marked by the imagination of its designers and, for the most part, its builders, is shown to us by the manifold examples still in existence: patent secretaries, ladies' writing tables, pillar bureaus, reading and writing pulpits, sewing, toilette and flower stands, card tables, etageres, servers, stove screens and many others.

In 1816 there were 875 independent master cabinetmakers in Vienna, in 1823 already 951. Some masters belonged to the guild; some were directly subordinate to the court. Some ran genuine factories. Probably the best-known and most influential of them was Josef Danhauser, who was already employing 100 workers in 1808.

In his "Establishment for all Objects of Furnishing", founded in 2804, he sold not only furniture produced in his factory, but home furnishings such as drapes, carpets, clocks and even glassware. The Austrian Museum of Applied Art has over 2500 of Danhauser's catalog drawings. They show an inclusive picture of the extent and types of production, the apparently never-ending fantasy of new shapes and decors. Danhauser also supplied designs that come alive in their straight lines and static tranquility, and shine through reduced to the constructive, without any decoration.

The fact that furniture can be identified as coming from this important factory on the basis of preserved drawings is rare. These pages reveal another important fact that characterizes the Vienna masters of that time: They were trained artists, for only those who had been trained in drawing for a specified length of time were allowed to take the master's test.

In private drawing schools, typified by that of Prussian-born Karl Schmidt, carpenters as well as other artisans could be trained and thus did not have to depend on designs from outsiders.

The government, despite its political position, was very interested in the further development of artisans and technicians in the new spirit of the times. In 1815 a new poly-technical school was opened; later it took over the contents of the product cabinet and also put the native products on exhibition in comparative competition. All of this allowed the Viennese furniture makers to work securely and solidly, which is reflected in the charming, imaginative home furnishings of the artisans' best quality.

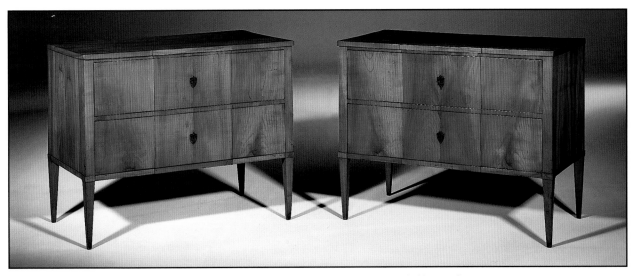

Pair of bureaus, Munich, circa 1805, Daniel Court Cabinetmakers.

Bavaria and Franconia

These fruitful prerequisites and fortunate circumstances in Vienna are found similarly expressed nowhere else in Germany. In Munich, for example, there were only 44 independent master cabinetmakers in 1822. At that time Munich was a small rural city in comparison with Augsburg or Nuremberg, and its court, especially under Ludwig I, followed classical style trends.

The active construction in Ludwig's reign resulted in a correspondingly stately style in rooms open to the public. The dominant architects *Friedrich von Gärtner* and *Leo von Klenze*, the latter also active in interior decoration, both worked in the courtly classic style. In the private "courtly" realm, "Biedermeier furniture," adopted by the well-to-do bourgeoisie, appeared after about 1805.

The merchant *Karl Ziller* took the first step of importance for handicrafts in 1816 when he founded a private polytechnic association. In the previous years he had already drawn attention to inventions and innovations, as well as problems of buying and selling, by publishing magazines and journals and putting on exhibitions in a hotel.

The confirmed pieces from this early era show simple yet noble forms. Legs and plates had to subordinate themselves to the often-seen strict flatness and are completely absorbed in a clear outline, set off at best by inlaid or painted-on ornamental bands. Cherry was the most commonly used veneer wood, followed by walnut, usually covering pine, but also beech.

Another characteristic of Munich furniture art can be seen in the graphics applied directly to the wood by transfer-printing, and decorating both outsides and interiors. This decorative process, known from its use on ceramics, was developed by *Johann Georg Hiltl*, who first displayed furniture decorated in this way at the exhibition of artistic and commercial products in 1818.

High-quality Biedermeier furniture was also made in the other south German cities which had already become known for furniture building in the 18th century. Augsburg, Nuremberg, Regensburg, Bamberg, Bayreuth, Würzburg and Ansbach must be noted as the most important centers. In Franconian furniture the underlying wood is usually pine. The makers and dates of some furniture owned by the Wittelsbach house can be determined.

Baden and Württemberg

In Karlsruhe, *Friedrich Weinbrenner*, and in Stuttgart and Ludwigsburg, *Nikolaus Friedrich Thonet* and *Johannes Klinckerfuss* had set the style of antique-oriented taste for courtly-elegant furnishings during the Empire era, and this was to affect the ensuing times. Considerable French influences are often recognizable in Baden.

Special forms were maintained particularly in the Lake Constance area. The veneer wood is usually cherry; in the vicinity of France walnut was used more often. Mahogany was preferred at the royal residences.

Mainz and Hesse

The center for the southwestern area was in Mainz, a city that in the 18th century had already produced splendid furniture that can be reckoned among the most beautiful examples of Baroque furniture art in Germany. A guild that was already progressive at that time, along with the French occupation, encouraged this outstanding position, which could be kept alive during the 19th and even into the 20th century.

Johann Wolfgang Kussmann, Wilhelm Kimbel and Philipp Anton Bembe and their furniture factories typify the great artisan tradition that made Mainz the most important center for the manufacture of Biedermeier furniture in the 19th century.

As early as 1816 there were more than 180 independent masters active there. Without guild pressure and with free enterprise, they found favorable conditions for a healthy competition. As a result of this blossoming of their work, exporting also increased steadily, as did the related style-forming inspiration of other nearby masters, workshops and regions. The Southwest and parts of Hesse were oriented to the Mainz products. Case furniture was dominated by the simple box form, reduced to the constructive, with a clearly visible cubic transparency. The desired flatness and optical unity resulted from the lively veined and knotted wood characteristic of this area; forming a completed veneer picture, it likewise covered angles, convexities and concavities and thus made them optically subordinate to the total picture. Set-in, flanking columns, often lacquered in black, added to the natural beauty of the veneer, often being its only decoration.

The masters also knew how to create those charming, imaginative small pieces that were not just a domain of the Viennese carpenters but also dominated by these masters. The fact may speak for itself that, for example, Wilhelm Kimbel, journeying before he opened his shop in 1815, had been to Vienna. Fine inlaid or painted-on tendril bands are found on projections, friezes, rows of columns, just as on the backs of chairs and benches.

The backs followed the bowed form, and the added decorations can be seen as transparent, clearly recognizable ornamentation. The preferred woods in this region were traditionally warm-toned cherry and walnut, mahogany and maple.

Saxony and Thuringia

In central Germany, Dresden, Leipzig and Erfurt became important, widely known furniture centers in the 18th century, building products of high quality. The stylistic influences that affected neighboring regions from these centers in the Biedermeier era can only be traced partially.

The central German furniture style is obviously a mixture of several style features. Styling influences from Brandenburg as well as Hesse and Austria-Bohemia can be seen. In Saxony and Saxony-Anhalt in particular, influences from Berlin can be recognized, as can the influence of Vienna, particularly in Saxony. And as early as 1816 an exhibition of Austrian products was held in Leipzig.

In western Thuringia, relationships with Hessian and Upper Franconian furniture styles can be found. These influences in both directions resulted from the usual travels of journeymen. In Thuringia and Saxony, individual furniture, some with makers' signatures, was also created.

The veneer woods were almost always cherry, walnut, mahogany and sometimes rosewood. After 1835, mahogany furniture was more often made with maple inlays in Saxony. Furniture was also made of massive ash.

Berlin

Berlin, capital and center of an important flatland state, experienced active construction in the Biedermeier years. The architect in charge of it, Karl Friedrich Schinkel, was responsible for both the building itself and the interior decor. As with Leo von Klenze, who was active in a comparable situation in Munich, Schinkel's designs show style elements of classicism and historicism.

For the court he created elegant furniture in late Empire style. But unlike Klenze, Schinkel also dealt steadily with the Biedermeier style in both architecture and furniture design. His masterful achievements in both are exemplified by, for example, the Academy of Building, built under his direction, in architecture and the very detailed design drawings created by him in the field of furniture.

The court cabinetmakers Johann Christian Sewening and Karl Georg Wandschaff produced much furniture to his designs. But Schinkel was just as interested in making his design drawings available to the many artisans in Berlin, of whom over 1300 masters and journeymen were registered there in 1816. This was done successfully from 1821 on, when he collaborated with State Counselor Wilhelm Christian Beuth to publish these drawings in the journal "Models for Factories and Artisans".

Typical of Schinkel's designs are the facades of furniture, which appear more splendid than elsewhere. The increased use of columns, architraves and other architectural elements, extending to simulated facades based on historical designs, plus the extraordinarily rich, for the Biedermeier era, ornamentation with antique-style decor elements, indicate the Empire style's comprehension of form.

Schinkel's excellent designs, created for the royalty and nobility, could be modified by artisans and thus made to fit the wishes of their customers. The carpenters, though, could just as well draw on comparatively simpler designs, if they could not create their own patterns. They found possibilities in the newly organized artisans' associations or private polytechnic organizations.

The accepted forms and decor of the north German area were also widely used in Berlin and Prussia. From 1800 to about 1820 there was quietly created mahogany furniture in "proto-Biedermeier style", which showed no elements of Empire and featured very richly composed interiors, often including marble columns.

The greater use of ornamental decor after 1835, as well as of maple fillet inlays in seating and container furniture may be regarded as cautious orientation clues to the localization of this furniture.

Other types of writing cabinets were usually made conically convergent toward the top. They paralleled mahogany furniture with quiet outlines. Birch was often used along with the very popular mahogany. Walnut and ash were also used. For the unseen wood of drawers, [p. 36] maple, linden and other hardwoods were sometimes used. Fire-gilded hardware was also used at times on court furniture.

As for the artistic quality of Berlin artisans' work, a noteworthy example is the patent secretary of Adolph Friedrich Voigt in the Museum of Commercial Art in Berlin. This impressive piece fulfills in a striking way the striving for functionality and mobility, whereby its maker clearly drew on a model illustrated in Thomas Sheraton's "Drawing Book". A writing cabinet signed and dated 1825 by Adolph F. Voigt is illustrated in this book, *(see #172, p. *135)*.

Pomerania and East Prussia

In Pomerania and East Prussia, more and more birch furniture appeared with very lively veneer patterns, often inspired by Brandenburg models.

Queen Louise's bedroom in Charlottenburg Palace, Berlin, the bed built in 1809-1810 to a design by Karl Friedrich Schinkel.

North Germany

North Germany, with its free Hanseatic cities, found other paths to Biedermeier style than those of the South. Since the Hanseatic cities were already organized as bourgeois communities in the 18th century, the courtly Empire style could never really extend or establish itself there, not even during the French occupation from 1810 to 1813.

The Biedermeier style developed from the "queue style" cultivated by the north German bourgeoisie, which in turn was clearly influenced by Britain and was very popular until the advent of Biedermeier itself. It was a direct stylistic continuation of development, in which influences of the heavy forms of Empire also entered in part.

In the North other woods were chosen for furniture making than in the South. The close trade relations with Britain and the settlements on the Caribbean islands and in South America made it possible to import mahogany easily, and this became the preferred wood of the north German cabinetmakers. Native birch, cherry, walnut and oak were also used. A folding-symmetrical veneer pattern is very common. Oak was almost always used for the underlying wood.

Container furniture usually had a strict cubic pattern. Writing cabinets often bore an architectonically formed top above the actual body, with several plates stepped one over the other. Such stepped tops also appeared on cupboards and showcases, in connection with gable designs or crowns.

Tops and completions with the most varied geometric forms, whether side by side or penetrating each other, were popular.

This play of contrasts is found in the decorative shapes inlaid in the surfaces, such as doorway arches, circles, squares, rectangles or rhombuses. Applied for accentuation, they could, for example, span two drawers, standing out in contrasting light and darkness, or serve as mounts for bronze hardware or painting. Another unique feature consisted of the stepped sliding panels that could also be applied in arched form.

The essential characteristics of Biedermeier furniture‾clarity, creation from the board and striving for flat surfaces‾are also native to this furniture. The latter refers to a panel often stretching between the feet in fan style, closing off the open socket space.

The British influence, more noticeable in furniture for sitting, can be recognized in terms of form by its restrained elegance as well as the use of typical British ornamentation. Tables with folding panels or sidepieces likewise have their models in the Anglo-Saxon realm, as do the many kinds of small furniture with which the bourgeoisie, thinking in terms of domesticity and livability, liked to surround itself. The political alliance of Altona and Schleswig-Holstein with Denmark inspired almost identical forms.

The Rhineland

The Rhineland and thus also the cabinetmakers of the lower Rhine were influenced from both Mainz and Frankfurt. The carved oak furniture that was once so cherished disappeared completely as courtly and upper-bourgeois furniture in the course of the Biedermeier era, as people turned to the now-modern veneered furniture.

Only rarely does one see carved parts, such as on chair and sofa backs or as table legs. Dolphins appear by preference, their portrayal likewise being adopted from the South, as well as horns of plenty or leaf designs.

North German style elements can also be recognized in this furniture as far as Westphalia, but they are used more as details than as definite complete forms. Cherry is especially popular as veneering, while ash was used more often in Westphalia.

Maintaining Value by Restoration and Care

Before examining techniques, details and materials, the basic tasks of restoration should be shown. The manner and thus the results of a restoration depend on the ability, experience and care of the restorer. Often furniture suffers from the inexperience or too-commercial approach of some restorers. Many pieces thus needlessly lose original substance and surface.

A restoration should always proceed from the individual piece. When the restorer knows this and subordinates himself to the object, the most important prerequisites for a correct restoration are at hand.

The highest law before the decision for a certain method is the attitude of the restorer to the condition in which the object is. He must suit his restorative and conservational measures to that.

The actual task of the restorer is the maintenance of the object of art. He often accepts faults and damage that can be removed only through a considerable loss of substance and originality. It should not be the restorer's job to put the furniture back into its original condition and give it a second new appearance. That way the real condition of a piece that has aged for a certain period of time would be falsified.

These natural signs of aging are just as important and justified a part of the object as its original appearance. A differentiation according to the condition of the piece is rather applied; but there are also "ruins" that are restorable in spite of everything.

The already described typical features, characteristics and innovations of this era have a direct effect on the restorer's work. This style also embodies a great number of characteristic types of damage. For the restorer this means mastery of a number of work processes specifically matched to this era, and their number is not to be underestimated, neither in technical or esthetic terms.

As for technique, it appears appropriate to lump furniture building from the late 18th century to the end of Biedermeier. In this period numerous technical developments became widespread, coming mainly from France and Britain and making their way to Germany. They were adopted by many cabinetmakers of the Biedermeier era and applied as new techniques.

In the esthetic formation and related characteristic damage, one can include Empire furniture. The similarly large-surface appearance of furniture of these two styles results in a related type of damage, especially in veneered pieces.

Therefore no specific collection of remedies specifically applicable to Biedermeier furniture can be compiled. The goal should be primarily a protective restoration. In addition, a small overview of the most commonly occurring dangers and damages should be offered, as well as sensible approaches and possible solutions.

Types of Damage

A restoration always begins with a thorough examination of the present condition of the furniture in question.

The following types of damage can be differentiated:

Damage to the construction of the body, frame, doors, surfaces and drawers

Damage to the surfaces of massively built furniture or veneered pieces.

Holes and cracks in the construction.

Holes in the veneer.

Damage to the veneer finish (paint, polish, wax or varnish)

Damage to the mechanics, such as bolts, bands, springs, locks and fittings (exclusively wooden mechanical damage seldom occurs)

Damage to other non-wood materials, such as colored paper drawer linings, leather on writing surfaces, cloth, part settings of ornaments (gilding, polychrome finish on caryatids, capitals, paw feet, etc.)

Damage to marquetry or intarsia with tin, brass, mother-of-pearl, ivory or other materials.

After examining the condition and determining the damage, the restorer must differentiate basically between conserving and restoring measures. By conserving is meant securing substances, maintaining the condition of the object and taking measures to prevent the occurrence of further damage.

Preservation

Protection from Vermin

The number one means of conserving furniture is prevention of attacks by wood-destroying insects. These are mainly the larvae of the deathwatch and related beetles *Annobiidae*. The larvae are capable of destroying the wood structure very quickly and almost completely without the extent of the damage being visible. Often we see an intact wood surface that, left standing paper-thin, conceals the real damage.

As a rule, the number of so-called tunnels of the *Annobiidae* gives an indication of the extent of the damage. Among these insects are the deathwatch and the furniture beetles. With very moist air and moderate room temperature, good conditions for the development of the larvae, their life cycle runs from May to August. Thus measures to avoid their damage should be taken just before that, when additional objects could be attacked. But it also should be remembered that a new attack scarcely ever occurs in modern apartments, buildings and collection rooms, since the climatic conditions there are usually not suitable. Coniferous woods are especially endangered.

In addition, the wood-destroying insects, especially the *Annobiidae*, have a fondness for animal albumen. For that reason, layers of glue or outer wood layers are usually more severely attacked than the actual wood.

The means of attacking these insects include gassing (only by a specialist!) and spraying a liquid medium. Liquids include oily chlornaphthalene wood-protection fluids and easily sprayed insecticides such as hexachlorcyclohexane and pentachlorphenol. Both should be applied only by the restorer, for when wrongly applied they can bring on a number of new damages. The health dangers that can occur are also very grave.

Aside from attacking the wood-damaging insects, a wood-solidifying means may also be used, depending on the destruction of the wood structure. Nowadays ethylcellulose and dissolving cellulose products are chiefly used; with their great penetrating depth, little danger of splitting which would cause new instability, and little inherent tension, they are far better suited to impregnating wood than epoxies and polyester resins.

Preservation of Structural Elements and Finishes

Conservation includes all those measures that serve to seal the furniture. One differentiates between sealing the constructive or massive body elements and sealing the veneer of furniture with veneering and marquetry.

In the body and frame, most damage results from the brittleness or decomposition of the animal glues also used in the first half of the 19th century. Animal adhesives become brittle mainly from aging and changing climatic conditions. Too little moisture in the air especially encourages this process and finally leads to the dissolution of the glue's firmness.

For that reason, extensive drying damage in the glued places occurs mainly in modern dwellings with far too little moisture in the air. Quickly changing degrees of moisture encourage this effect, since moistening and drying of the glue take place very quickly, taking away much of its elasticity.

As opposed to brittleness, animal glue is also attacked by decomposition bacteria at humidity levels over 65 percent, also in masses glued together. The damage is similar to that of brittleness but sometimes requires different measures. This has two consequences for attaching and gluing. It is possible to expand animal glues and increase their adhesive power with heat and humidity, which does not necessarily make the application of additional glue necessary; it is known as "regenerating" the glue. If the glue already present is not sufficient, the addition of heated glue is necessary. This technique is used mainly in reattaching loose pieces of furniture, to remove the air pockets that have formed under the veneer.

In gluing constructive elements such as bottoms, sides, frame, pegs, dovetails and the like, cracks in fillings and other details, a complete regluing is often necessary, since high demands are made on the lime here. At this point it is an open question whether animal or white glues should be used, since the necessity of making a measure reversible in such operations must not necessarily be made the rule.

In such cases the necessity of conserving is of primary importance.

Preservation of the Wood Surfaces

The question of surface treatment, when a surface can be regenerated, is also part of the conservative measures for a piece of furniture. The original main task of the treatment of a wood surface is to protect it from damage, dirt and climatic influences. Only second in rank is the desire for an esthetic exterior. Thus the choice of the surface material should unite these two components.

A very early surface treatment known to us today is the use of waxes and wax balsams. Only much later were so-called resin lacquers developed, in which, especially in the 18th century, stronger and stronger combinations of various resins were blended. They have increased requirements to fulfill in terms of surface protection, color tones, degrees of hardness, transparency, workability and finally polishing ability.

A comparatively new material is shellac, made of tree lice from India; its use became widespread in the Biedermeier era. The very high degree of surface hardness, the quick drying of this lacquer, influenced by the use of alcohol as a solvent, and the related relatively quick workability gave it its great popularity at that time.

Among conserving viewpoints, though, there are differences, because of the high degree of hardness, which offers very great protection from mechanical damage, for with changes of climatic conditions, especially dryness, capillary cracks in the polish may occur.

Thus the surface proves to be considerably more sensitive to an unfavorable room climate and thus is destroyed slowly. This is much less the case with more elastic lacquers, and much less noticeable. In this type of surface damage, cleaning and over-polishing of the disintegrating layer of lacquer can be helpful. Similar, more refined techniques should be used as a test on serious lacquer damage, larger craquelé surfaces of light damage (pale, nontransparent lacquer appearance), before the restorer too hastily removes an old surface coating.

A comparison between dirty and cleaned lacquer.

An aged polish or surface belongs to the historical appearance of a piece of furniture just as much as the rest of its appearance. Therefore the surface and the finish should be given the same attention as has long since been devoted with the greatest understanding to paintings and sculptures.

The restorer must also understand in this situation that a removed or even halfway retained surface means a loss of value, which is just as costly to Biedermeier furniture as to valuable older pieces from the 17th and 18th centuries.

Unfortunately, the practice of removing substance worth retaining from a surface with the most radical methods, by grinding and lacquering anew, is still widespread in present-day furniture restoring. Despite all our experience, such radical methods are still justified by an easier sale of the pieces. For that reason, the buyer of such furniture should be urged to change his concept of taste with respect to the furniture and not try to obtain "immaculate" highly polished items. It should be clear to every interested person that well-kept original Biedermeier furniture keeps becoming rarer, and that this brings about its increased value.

Proper Maintenance Protects Against Damage

Finally, every conserving or restoring measure, no matter how right or how well done, is only going to last as long as climatic conditions allow. It is incorrectly assumed that temperature changes cause wood or dryness damage. These depend exclusively on the climatic conditions—particularly the degree of humidity in the air.

It is possible, though, to have varied room temperatures as long as the degree of humidity in the air is kept constant. The ideal range lies between 45 and 55 percent. To keep such percentages relatively constant for years and thus to do what one can for conservation as an owner of antique furniture, one needs a humidifier, especially in postwar or new buildings.

With modern heating systems it is usually impossible to create such conditions in any other way. Thus the humidity during a period of heating usually amounts to between 25 and 40 percent.

Thus the dryness damage noted above is bound to occur. The wood "works" under these conditions; large-scale damage occurs through shrinking and splintering. When one keeps in mind that wood can shrink in a humidity change from 50 to 20 up to 10 percent across the grain and up to 5 percent radially (in the direction from the core of the wood toward the bark), it must become clear that even very careful designs that should decrease shrinking damage and avoid splitting can be incapable of preserving wood from extensive damage.

The most commonly occurring types of damage to Biedermeier furniture may be listed as follows:
shrinking of massive plates
loosening of pieces glued to a board
loosening of drawer fronts
shrinking of fillings in a frame (sometimes to the point of falling out)
shrinking of frame elements (especially those in Biedermeier that were smoothed and veneered over, so that cracks occur along the line of shrinkage in the veneer)
loosening of veneer through glue degeneration. Veneered parts of the body in particular suffer characteristic veneer damage from shrinkage of dovetails and result in breakage that is often hard to repair.

How to Avoid Damage

Biedermeier furniture, on account of the aforementioned stylistic construction and design, is very sensitive to excessively humid air. Shrinkage cracks that run through the veneer are very noticeable and can detract from the entire appearance and thus from the esthetics of the veneer appearance. In baroque furniture with rich marquetry this is usually not so noticeable, since shrinkage cracks often occur at veneer junctions where a change is wanted anyway.

Aside from mechanical humidifying, every owner of Biedermeier furniture can take additional measures to avoid shrinkage damage: not overheating the rooms, which takes too much moisture out of the furniture. Furniture should never be placed right next to stoves or radiators.

Incorrect ventilation can result in a climate collapse that often results in direct damage. Direct sunshine on the furniture is absolutely to be avoided. It cannot be in the best interests of the owner to find the same damage occurring to furniture that has recently been restored. The restorer is not to be held responsible for this, for he had no influence on unfavorable climatic conditions.

Rather it is more appropriate to become mistrustful when restorers suggest measures with which such damage can be avoided. Often these amount to "impregnating all sides with artificial resins", "lacquering with non-yellowing artificial resin lacquers", and so on, these being not at all practical conserving measures that have no effect on the substance of the object.

Restoration

Dealing with Bad Spots

The most important standpoint of a restorative measure is the removal of holes in the structure, body, show sides, veneer and frame.

Holes in the structure are mechanically caused splits, breaks, splinters and destruction of wood connections or damage resulting from wear on drawers, doors, panels and other moving parts. Usually this damage can be repaired by simply filling of the wood.

Sometimes the replacement or completion of individual parts is necessary.

These generally concern foot pegs, dovetails, pegs, runners, drawer bottoms, back-wall and bottom attachments (especially in Biedermeier furniture), as well as dovetails and swallowtails in swallowtail connections, bow-shaped inlaid cylinder pieces of the popular Biedermeier cylinder secretaries, and other more rarely occurring structural details.

Repairing Wood Breakage

In the body, the restorer's main task is dealing with shrinkage damage. Usually these are cracks in the board-glued large-surface body parts or shrinkage cracks in the smooth frame elements.

This damage occurs in Biedermeier furniture very often and often destroys the appearance of entire show sides. If cracks cannot be eliminated by filling them with glue, then a strip of wood is usually set in along the crack. For that reason the restorer who deals with this kind of damage should be well versed in such work. One also needs, in setting a strip of wood in, to have a good eye for the color and structure of the wood. Every repair shows clearly by retouching the color, since the impression of a unified flat surface is much disturbed if the retouched area stands out.

Closing and fixing such shrinkage cracks from the rear is very much to be discouraged if the restored piece is not to be placed immediately in a regulated climate, since crack fillings done in this way usually split in another place from renewed drying and resulting shrinkage. It is better to accept a crack in the same place in the bargain, and thus no additional substance is lost.

Likewise, dovetailed or slotted-in moldings should not be glued. This too is frequently tried in order to prevent cracks. This measure is completely useless. Shrinkage cracks basically occur due to dryness and cannot be avoided thus.

Replacement of Missing Parts

Through the formation of the show sides already discussed elsewhere, often resulting from single elements such as blocks, cubes, friezes and other geometrical wooden elements, the loss of these glued parts

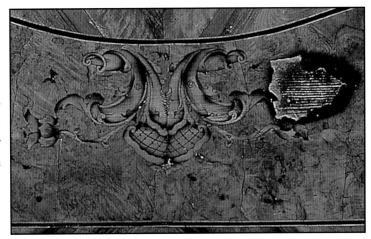

A burn hole in the veneer

from outside influence on the gluing is very high. If these elements can be reconstructed on the basis of their glue traces, the restorer of Biedermeier furniture can often do carpentry work in its own sense.

The requirements in the creation of profiles, circle segments, arcs, columns, capitals, toothed friezes, posts, balustrades, legs, feet and many others are rich in variations and require great skill and sufficient experience from the restorer of the more elaborate furniture.

Veneer Damage

In the restoration of veneer damage, the restorer of Biedermeier furniture is tested extraordinarily. While in 18th-century marquetry furniture the difficulty was limited to filling in gaps with the right choice of wood, in the case of these veneer patterns that extend over the whole surface, the filling of gaps must fit into the often very impressive pattern quietly and harmoniously, and do so along with the often broken crosspieces of the drawers, traverses, doors and writing panels just as with the over-veneered wood joints. Here too, along with the right restoration of the damage, a good retouching is a prerequisite for repairs that disturb the optical impression as little as possible.

In the repairing of wood damage, every restorative job should be carried out so that the intact periphery of the damaged place will not be disturbed. Grinding and smoothing with the involvement of the neighboring areas are measures to be avoided, as is the unnecessary removal of the surface. Whoever cannot make repairs without losing the patina should avoid restoration altogether.

The original inlaid escutcheons of hard-sliding drawers often suffer damage.

Thus after expert treatment of all damage, after the surface has been treated carefully, including the usually employed lock shields of ebony, bone or mother-of-pearl, a characteristic large-surface harmony is achieved, which makes Biedermeier furniture come alive.

When every conservative and restorative measure is determined by the character of the furniture, and every measure is taken by the respectfully working, experienced and specialist worker with as little loss of substance as possible, the furniture regains its significance in furniture history.

From the beginning of every restoration, the restorer must be aware of this important task.

Tips, Trends and Market Tendencies

In the early days of its discovery as collectors' items, between 1960 and 1970, Biedermeier furniture was very reasonably priced, and the tendency to obtain entire room sets prevailed.

Since the beginning of the 1990s, the trend goes more and more toward striking, high-quality individual pieces, functional and beautiful furniture that should often form a deliberate contrast to modern furnishing. It is good to see a growing desire for original furniture with a historically developed patina, as opposed

Reconstruction of the floor created by Leo von Klenze in the king's workroom in the Munich Residence.

to the earlier preference for furniture that was often overly restored.

As for the popularity of certain types of furniture, the first place is held by dining groups and sets of chairs, as well as container furniture, since they combine functionality and esthetics effectively. The writing cabinet might be mentioned first here, but showcases, cupboards and bureaus are also very sought-after. The writing cabinet, or secretary, offers a high degree of functionality, storage space and financial value. Often a writing cabinet, cupboard and sofa form the basis of a room's furnishings and are completed in time with additional furniture.

In Biedermeier furniture, as elsewhere, it is true that particular quality has its price. Extraordinary and elaborate shapes, high-quality decorations and masterly work and sought and have their effect on prices. Special furniture of the "Vienna School" is very expensive because of these qualities. Very high prices are paid for imaginative individual pieces such as globe tables and lyre secretaries.

Sets of seating furniture, including sets of chairs, are much more expensive than the individual pieces. A very good condition, especially of the surfaces, also demands a high price.

The light wood of the cherry tree is presently most popular, followed by walnut and mahogany. Woods such as ash, oak and birch are less desired and thus less expensive as a rule. Particularly high-value objects were often made of mahogany for royal residences.

A condition that requires restoration (see also the notes in the catalog section and price guide) usually call for a much lower price. If you want to purchase a piece, you should keep the following in mind when you make a decision:

The furniture must please you optically and in terms of size.

It should be in an extensively original condition, for major restoration lowers the value.

Make the purchase either in a reliable specialty shop or at an auction with an expert catalog description.

If possible, compare various offerings before you make the purchase.

Inform yourself as to the possible cost of restoration.

In case of doubt, consult a neutral specialist.

An increase in value of beloved Biedermeier furniture is possible as in the past, but should not be decisive in the decision to buy. Unlike new furniture, which loses value rapidly after being purchased, Biedermeier furniture should at least maintain its value.

Catalog Illustration Section

Notes on the Catalog Section and Price Guide

If one concentrates on one stylistic epoch in compiling a furniture catalog, it is advantageous to organize it according to the various types of furniture. Thus the most important furniture types of the Biedermeier era will be presented hereafter in a representative choice of regionally varying forms, with description and dating.

The selection of photos reflects the present-day art market as well as that of the most recent years. Nearly all the pieces are or were offered either in auctions or in the antique trade. The stated values are based almost exclusively on the actual sale prices in the antique trade. For furniture that was auctioned, restoration costs, if any, have been included.

Yet a varied standard of prices exists between auctions and specialty shops. The trade often carefully offers a selection of special pieces. The cost-reflecting workmanship and possible time on sale and financing must be considered in the sales price. Thus the customer has the pleasure of not having to make a decision under pressure and of being dealt with individually. Usually a trial placement within his own four walls is possible.

As a rule, the auction house cannot offer such service, which often results in more reasonable prices. The legal and contractual liability for faults or assured qualities is often quite different between antique shops and auction houses.

To make the difference that exists in the evaluation of Biedermeier furniture clearer, a price span is given in the price guide. Different calculations and cost situations result in a differentiated price range in specialty shops.

Many market mechanisms, plus fashions and personal preferences, determine the market activity. In the art trade the old rule is: "A work of art is always worth what is paid for it."

If you should want to sell a piece, aim for about half of the stated purchase price. This applies to the specialty trade as well as the serious auction trade, which often reaches an international public through its superbly prepared catalogs.

Trade terminology is explained in a glossary in the appendix, after the photo section. Often, though, the sense of a trade term becomes clearer from comparing the description with the picture, or of the pictures with each other.

Furniture Trademarks

1

2

3

4

5

6

7

8

9

10

Signed or dated furniture is very rare in the Biedermeier era, as also in the 18th century. In the German lands there was no legal requirement to sign furniture or identify it otherwise. Signatures are found somewhat more often on journeymen's or masters' qualifying works. Often not only the place of manufacture (8), but also the master's birthplace, sometimes very different, is stated.

The pencil signature is the most common type of signature (1, 2, 3, 4, 7, 8). Usually this is applied in an obscure place and therefore often is overlooked.

Bureau, circa 1830, Vienna, walnut, core wood, inside drawers with fronts of
cherry, two doors, drawers inside, originally fire-gilded bronze hardware. 80 cm
high, 125 wide, 52 deep. $13,000-14,000. 13,500 E

Two Bureaus, circa 1805, Munich, Daniel Court Cabinetmakers,
cherry, two drawers, inlaid shield-shaped escutcheons. 84 cm
high, 100 wide, 52 deep. Together $16,000-19,000. 17,000 E

Bureau, circa 1820, Franconia, cherry, 3 drawers, flanked by
inset ebonized half-columns, ebonized edges, inlaid shield-
shaped escutcheons. 88 mm high, 87 wide, 45 deep. $6,500-
7,000. 7,000 E

Chiffonier, circa 1815, Vienna, mahogany, pilasters with busts above, Egyptian-style caryatids, seven drawers, original brass hardware, brass palm decorations, brass bands all around. 136 mm high, 51 wide, 36 deep. $11,000-12,000. 11,500 E

Writing Cabinet, circa 1815, Vienna, pear, maple, ash, black polish, ebonized body, two doors below, several drawers behind them, black-lead painting, top drawer, original fire-gilded bronze hardware. 156 mm high, 94 wide, 46 deep. $18,000-19,500. 19,000 E

Writing Cabinet, circa 1820, Austria, walnut, poplar and birch root, three drawers below, flanking columns set in at the sides, writing panel, behind it central tempietto with three mirrors, surrounded by drawers, four columns, black-lead painting on the top and bottom, secret compartments, top drawer, gablelike top, original fire-gilded bronze hardware. 165 mm high, 99 wide, 49 deep. $29,000-32,500. 31,000 E

Writing Cabinet, circa 1840, Saxony, cherry, mahogany, maple marquetry, three drawers below, flanking thin double columns, writing panel, behind it several drawers with marquetry, central drawer flanked by two columns, top drawer, stepped top with cushion on top, inlaid four-cornered escutcheons. 180 mm high, 105 wide, 60 deep. $17,500-19,500. 19,000 E

Writing Cabinet, circa 1815, Munich, cherry, alder root, maple, two drawers below, flanking ebonized columns set at the sides, gilded capitals and bases, writing panel, several drawers behind it, very rich central area with mirrors, silver and gold painting, three stamped-on color lithographs, ebonized columns, top drawer, architectonically rich top with many columns and arches, triangular gable as crown. 186 mm high, 97 wide, 53.5 deep. $125,000-140,000. 133,000 E

The cabinet shown on page 56, opened.

Writing Cabinet, circa 1805, Berlin, signed Ruppert, clock signed Kleemeier, mahogany and other woods, two doors below writing panel flanked by two alabaster columns, several drawers, central niche with steps, two mirrored doors above, four steps above, with clock flanked by two alabaster columns, Arabic numerals, triangular gable. $90,000-110,000. 100,000 E

Writing Cabinet, circa 1810, Berlin, mahogany, maple, lemon, two drawers below, writing panel, several drawers behind it, top drawer, top with triangular gable, inlaid oval ivory escutcheons. 165 mm high, 95 wide, 40 deep. $14,000-16,000. 15,000 E

Lyre Secretary,
Frankfurt, signed
Friedrich Marschal
Master 1832 in
Frankfurt, mahoga[...]
veneered on oak,
maple, root wood,
lower body narrows
drawer, writing pan[...]
above it, very ornat[...]
interior with drawe[...]
four white columns,
bases and settings,
triangular gable in
central niche, steps
and parquet marqu[...]
try, numerous iron
mechanisms for sec[...]
and spring drawers,
large top drawer
made as lectern wit[...]
further drawer
division, stepped to[...]
165 mm high, 104
wide, 52 deep.
$90,000-110,000.
100,000 E

The cabinet shown on page 60, opened.

Cupboard, circa 1820, Austria, walnut, two outside doors, flanking ebonized
columns with gilded bases and capitals, ebonized bottom apron, top cornice.
$10,000-11,500. 11,000 E

Half-cupboard, circa 1810, Vienna, black lacquered body, one door, flanking
pilasters, top drawer, original fire-gilded bronze hardware. 152 cm high, 65 wide,
38 deep. $13,500-14,500. 14,000 E

Cupboard, circa 1825, southern Germany, two doors, flanking ebonized columns, ebonized pieces, top cornice. $8,500-10,000. 9,000 E

Cupboard, circa 1820, eastern Bavaria, two doors, flanking ebonized
columns, ebonized parts, top cornice. $7,000-8,500. 8,000 E

Cupboard, circa 1815, Westphalia, massive and veneered cherry, ebony intarsia, oak frame, two drawers below, cornice gable, inlaid ebonized four-cornered escutcheons, stamped brass applications on the pilasters. 208 cm high, 201 wide, 73 deep. $19,000-21,000. 20,000 E

Opposite page: **Bookcase,** Vienna, signed Albrecht 1825, receipted Erstes Wiener Möbelheim I, cherry, two doors, glassed above, richly branched round arches, lower rectangular bars, angled cornice. 245 cm high, 164 wide 48 deep. $27,500-30,000. 29,000 E

Bookcase, circa 1820, Nuremberg, cherry, pear, two doors, mirrored above, paneled below, triangular gable, flanking ebonized columns. 182 cm high, 125 wide, 40.5 deep. $18,500-20,000. 19,000 E

Bookcase, circa 1815, Weimar, massive and veneered mahogany, two doors, glassed above with oval and diagonal bars, paneled below with diamond patterns, original brass hardware. 162 cm high, 92 wide, 32 deep. $11,000-12,500. 12,000 E

Showcase, circa 1825, Berlin, mahogany, glassed doors, flanking columns with gilded capitals and bases, bottom drawers with two diamond-shaped cutouts. 177 cm high, 90 wide, 50 deep. $12,500-14,000. 13,000 E

Table, circa 1820, designed by Josef Danhauser, Vienna,
mahogany, maple, oval top, two channeled legs tapered
downward, round sockets with link. 79 cm high, 145 wide, 72.5
deep. $24,000-27,500. 26,000 E

Table, circa 1810, Austria, mahogany, foot of three bound
snakes, partly gilded, partly green, round top, three-pointed
socket. $19,000-20,000. 20,000 E

Table, circa 1830, Baden, walnut, some of it crosscut, star-shaped veneered top, central baluster column, three-pointed foot with three scrolls. $7,000-8,500. 8,000 E

Small Table, circa 1825, Brandenburg, birch root, round top, ten-pointed socket plate,
columnar foot on cubic base, drawer in rim. 75 cm high, 62 diameter. $3,250-3,750. 3,500 E

Decorative Table, circa 1805, Vienna, mahogany veneer on maple and fir, mahogany and etched pear marquetrypartly gilded carved legs, original hardware, four winged female figures in Egyptian style surround central foot tapering in at the middle. 76.5 cm high, 58 wide, 44 deep. $30,000-37,500. 33,750 E

Writing Table, circa 1815, Neuwied, attributed to Johann Wilhelm Vetter, cherry veneer on fir
(body) and oak (drawers), four drawers below, writing panel, drawers and doord above, adjustable-
height top with writing and note lectern, crank operates three work processes, raising and lowering
as well as lectern structure, 21 oak drawers in all, seven secret compartments—some with springs
and hidden mechanisms, six drawers above, four-sided pointed legs, unusually precisely worked
locks and multiple bolting, original brass hardware and pull rings. 145 cm high, 133 wide, 66 deep.
$32,500-37,500. 35,000 E

The desk shown on page 76, opened.

Five Chairs, circa 1805, Regensburg, originally from prince-bishop's residence there, later Ringler family, walnut massive and veneered on pine, original upholstery and beading, inventory numbers R 15. R 23, R 24 written on beading, front rims veneered with mirrors over central panel, Gothic-style fence in lower part of back, back rims of massive walnut, showing that the chairs were made to be seen from the front (placed along room walls), of the original upholstery only the hand-woven beadings and linen covering remain. Set for $19,000-21,000. 20,000 E

Two Fancy Armchairs, circa 1805, Regensburg, cherry on soft wood and beech, originally mahoganized, polished, two front legs made like one-pawed lions, supporting arms, probably carved by the Regensburg sculptor Christoph Itelsperger, 1763-1842, original fire-gilded bronze fittings, original beading and bourlet, high-class armchairs often had heavy fringe. 91.3 and 91.1 cm high, 57.5 and 60 wide, 65.5 deep. Pair for $90,000-95,000. 92,500 E

Sofa, circa 1815, Vienna, mahogany, carved arms, partly gilded dolphins,
reconstructed original upholsery, legs of intersecting semicircles. 89 cm
high, 154 wide, 70 deep. $20,000-22,000. 21,000 E

Sofa, circa 1825, upper Bavaria, cherry, curved back and arms.
103 cm high, 196 wide, 70 deep. $7,500-8,500. 8,000 E

1

2

3

1. Bureau, circa 1805, Vienna, pear, black polished, three drawers, two partly gilded caryatids flanking the two lower drawers, original fire-gilded hardware, lion's-paw feet. 90 cm high, 110 wide, 57 deep. $30,000-32,500. 31,000 E

2. Bureau, circa 1810, Vienna, walnut root wood, four drawers, two partly gilded carved busts flanking the two middle drawers, original fire-gilded hardware. 98 cm high, 114 wide, 58 deep. $17,000-19,000. 18,000 E

3. Pair of Bureaus, circa 1815, Vienna, walnut, three drawers, two partly gilded carved busts flanking the two lower drawers, original stamped brass hardware. $22,500-27,500. 25,000 E

4

5

4. Bureau, circa 1815, Austria, cherry, swamp oak, ebony, four drawers, projecting top drawer, two partly gilded conical busts flanking the two middle drawers, original stamped brass hardware. 94 cm high, 127 wide, 63 deep. $10,000-13,000. 12,000 E

5. Bureau, circa 1815, Austria, cherry, three drawers, projecting top drawer with frieze of tendrils, original stamped brass hardware. 85.3 cm high, 118 wide, 57.5 deep. $8,500-10,000. 9,000 E

6. Bureau, circa 1815, Austria, cherry, three drawers, projecting top drawer, partly gilded carved bust pilasters flanking the three lower drawers, inlaid shield-shaped escutcheons. 89 cm high, 130 wide, 67 deep. $11,000-13,000. 12,000 E

6

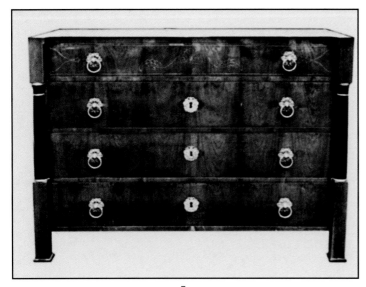

7

8

9

7. Bureau, circa 1830, Bohemia, walnut, four drawers, flanking ebonized columns, closing plate projecting on the sides, geometrical and floral marquetry with central shell shapes in maple. 88 cm high, 118 wide, 60 deep. $4,500-5,500. 5,000 E

8. Bureau, circa 1830, Austria, walnut core wood, three drawers, flanking ebonized columns, original brass hardware, the repeated veneer pattern unites the bureau optically. 90 cm high, 125 wide, 60 deep. $4,000-4,500. 4,500 E

9. Bureau, circa 1830, Vienna, walnut, including heartwood, drawers inside with cherry front, two doors, drawers inside, original fire-gilded bronze hardware. 80 cm high, 125 wide, 52 deep. $13,000-14,000. 13,500 E

10

11

10. Bureau, circa 1835, Upper Austria, cherry, three drawers, mostly original stamped brass hardware. 85.5 cm high, 122 wide, 61.5 deep. $3,500-4,000. 4,000 E

11. Bureau, circa 1830, Austria, cherry, three drawers, ebonized edges, stamped brass hardware. 84 cm high, 120 wide, 58 deep. $5,750-6,500. 6,000 E

12. Bureau, circa 1835, Austria, walnut, three drawers, inlaid ebonized shield-shaped escutcheons. 83 cm high, 121 wide, 56 deep. $3,750-4,5,000. 4,000 E

12

13

14

15

13. Two Bureaus, circa 1805, Munich, Daniel Court Cabinetmakers, cherry, two drawers, inlaid shield-shaped escutcheons. 84 cm high, 100 wide, 52 deep. Pair $16,000-19,000. 13,000 E

14. Bureau, circa 1810, Munich, Daniel Court Cabinetmakers, cherry, two drawers, black shadowlines on upper and lower edges of the body, ebonized inlaid shield-shaped escutcheons. 86 cm high, 109.5 wide, 55 deep. $7,000-8,000. 7,500 E

15. Bureau, circa 1810, Munich, Daniel Court Cabinetmakers, cherry, black etched maple and ebony, stripe inlay all around, inlaid shield-shaped escutcheons of ebony. 80 cm high, 115 wide, 56 deep. $7,000-8,000. 7,500 E

16

17

In Biedermeier furniture the escutcheons are often inlaid. The drawer is pulled by the key in order to leave the chosen veneer pattern unspoiled and not interrupted by hardware. Just as often, drawer handles and escutcheons are made of sheet brass pressed into a model.
The plate form fully integrated into the outline of furniture from Upper Bavaria can be regarded as a regional characteristic.

16 Bureau, circa 1820, Upper Bavaria, cherry, ribbon inlay all around, two drawers, inlaid shield-shaped ebonized lock shields. 83 cm high, 105 wide, 52 deep. $5,500-6,000. 6,000 E

17 Bureau, circa 1815, Upper Bavaria, cherry, three drawers, inlaid diamond-shaped lock shields. 86 cm high, 122 wide, 64 deep. $5,000-6,000. 5,500 E

18. Two Bureaus, circa 1830, southern Germany, walnut, three drawers. 84 cm high, 99 wide, 52 deep. Pair $10,000-12,000. 11,000 E

18

19

20

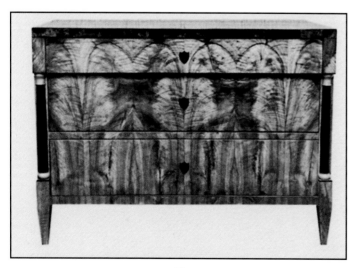

21

19. Bureau, circa 1820, Upper Bavaria, cherry, three drawers, flanking ebonized half-columns, inlaid ebonized shield-shaled escutcheons. 86 cm high, 121 wide, 56 deep. $6,000-6,500. 6,000 E

20. Bureau, circa 1820, Upper Bavaria, cherry, three drawers, flanking ebonized columns, gilded capitals and bases, upper drawer black with flowers and tendrils, inlaid shield-shaped escutcheons. 92 cm high, 130 wide, 40 deep. $9,000-10,000. 9,500 E

21. Bureau, circa 1820, Upper Bavaria, walnut, three drawers, flanking ebonized half-columns, top set off with border all around, choice veneer pattern. 86 cm high, 117 wide, 58 deep. $4,500-5,500. 4,500 E

22

23

22. Bureau, circa 1830, southern Germany, cherry, three drawers, flanking ebonized half-columns. 90 cm high, 128 wide, 65 deep. $4,000-4,750. 4,000 E

23. Bureau, circa 1835, southern Germany, crosscut walnut, three drawers, stamped brass hardware with figured motifs. 86 cm high, 115 widw, 56 deep. $3,250-4,000. 3,500 E

24. Bureau, signed in pencil on the back, made by Master Cabinetmaker Pattinger in Tittmoning, 1850, walnut, three drawers, stamped brass hardware. 91 cm high, 120 wide, 62 deep. $3,000-3,500. 3,000 E

24

25

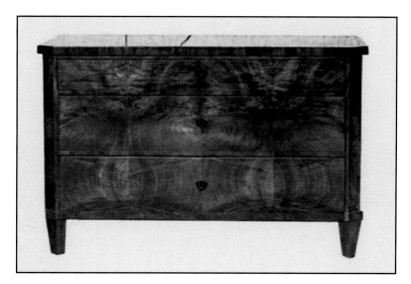

26

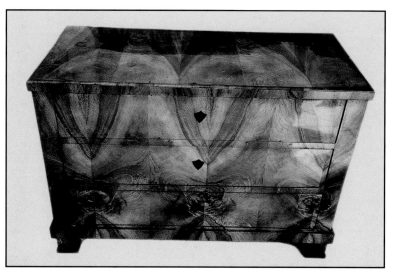

27

25. Bureau, circa 1810, Baden, cherry, walnut including crosscut, rail maple, knotty maple, swamp oak, pear, three drawers, line and ball marquetry, inlaid shield-shaped escutcheons. 86 cm high, 119.5 wide, 63 deep. $8,000-9,000. 8,500 E

26 Bureau, circa 1815, southwestern Germany, walnut, three drawers. 84 cm high, 74 wide, 51 deep. $3,000-3,500. 3,500 E

27. Bureau, circa 1820, Upper Swabia, walnut, three drawers, inlaid shield-shaped ebonized escutcheons. 84 cm high, 90 wide, 58 deep. $4,000-4,500. 4,000 E

28

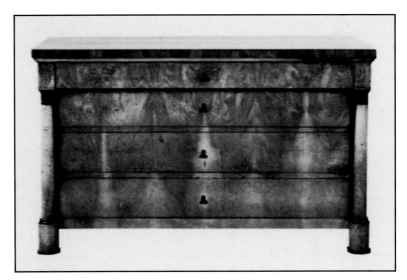

29

28. Bureau, circa 1820, Baden, walnut, two drawers, flanking ebonized pilasters, inlaid shield-shaped escutcheons. 75 cm high, 80 wide, 48 deep. $6,000-6,500. 6,500 E

29. Bureau, circa 1825, southwestern Germany, walnut, four drawers, projecting top drawer, flanking columns becoming rounded feet. $4,000-4,500. 4,500 E

30. Bureau, dated made in March 1845 by Bernhard Füsslein, southwestern Germany, cherry, three drawers, flanking side columns, brass lock insets. 78 cm high, 102 wide, 54.5 deep. $6,000-7,000. 6,500 E

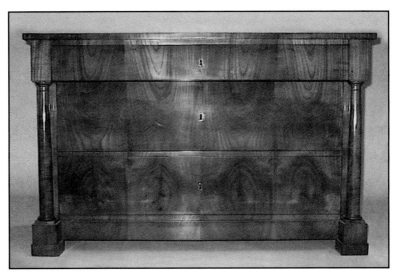

30

31

32

33

Ebonizing or blackening was done to imitate expensive ebony wood.

31. Bureau, circa 1805, Franconia, cherry, three drawers, brand and inventory stamps. 88 cm high, 87 wide, 45 deep. $6,000-7,000. 6,500 E

32. Bureau, circa 1820, Franconia, pear, black polished body, two drawers, inlaid diamond-shaped bone escutcheons. 78 cm high, 89 wide, 49 deep. $5,500-6,500. 6,000 E

33. Bureau, circa 1820, Franconia, cherry, three drawers, flanking ebonized half-columns, upper drawer adorned with horizontal cut diamond shape, inlaid diamond-shaped escutcheons. 90 cm high, 122 wide, 58 deep. $7,500-8,500. 8,000 E

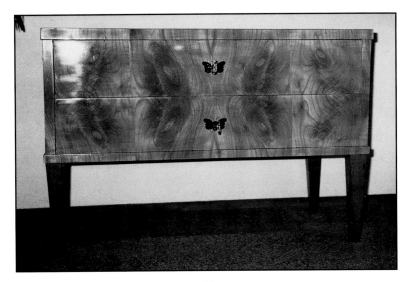

34

35

34. Bureau, circa 1815, Würzburg, Martin Eyrich, cherry, two drawers, inlaid butterfly-shaped escutcheons. 76 cm high, 80 wide, 46 deep. $8,000-8,500. 8,000 E

35. Bureau, circa 1830, Franconia, cherry, three drawers, flanking ebonized half-columns, gold-finished bases and capitals. 84.5 cm high, 104 wide, 56.5 deep. $6,500-7,000. 6,500 E

36. Bureau, circa 1830, Franconia, cherry, three drawers, flanking ebonized half-columns and edges, inlaid shield-shaped escutcheons. 88 cm high, 87 wide, 45 deep. $6,500-7,000. 6,500 E

36

37

38

39

37. Bureau, circa 1830, Franconia, cherry, three drawers, flanking ebonized columns with gilded bases and capitals, inlaid ebonized escutcheons. $6,000-7,000. 6,500 E

38. Bureau, circa 1830, Lower Franconia, cherry, cherry root, three drawers, flanking ebonized half-columns, inlaid shield-shaped escutcheons. 82 cm high, 111.5 wide, 57 deep. $5,500-6,500. 6,000 E

39. Bureau, signed Peter Olt, journeyman cabinetmaker, Königsfeld (Lower Franconia), dated 1840, walnut, poplar root, three drawers, flanking ebonized half-columns, inlaid diamond-shaped escutcheons. 87 cm high, 109 wide, 55 deep. $7,000-8,000. 7,500 E

40

40. Bureau, circa 1830, southwestern
Franconia, walnut, three drawers, flanking
ebonized columns, diamond-shaped escutcheons. 85 cm high, 118.5 wide, 63 deep.
$6,000-7,000. 7,000 E

41. Bureau, circa 1820, Franconia, cherry, three
drawers, under the projecting top drawer are
two flanking ebonized columns. $4,500-5,500.
5,000 E

41

42

43

42. Bureau, circa 1825, western Thuringia, cherry, cherry root, three drawers, flanking ebonized columns. 84 cm high, 120 wide, 59 deep. $4,500-5,500. 5,000 E

43. Bureau, dated 1815, Jena, signed Johann Müller, veined poplar, maple, mahogany, three drawers, 76 cm high, 97 wide, 46.5 deep. $6,000-6,500. 6,500 E

44. Bureau, circa 1825, Thuringia, walnut, maple root, three drawers, arched front field, inlaid shield-shaped escutcheons. 86 cm high, 112 wide, 55 deep. $6,000-6,500. 6,500 E

45. Bureau, circa 1825, Thuringia, birch, birch root, three drawers, slightly projecting base, prismatic corner indentations, cut-in arch segment, accented by birch-root wood on middle drawer. 84 cm high, 107 wide, 56 deep. $4,400-4,900. 4,500 E

46. Bureau, circa 1820, Thuringia, maple, three drawers, upper drawer with ebonized arch segment. $6,000-6,500. 6,000 E

44

45

46

47

48

49

The breaking of the choice mahogany veneer pattern with maple fillets was very popular, particularly in Berlin, but also in Saxony and North Germany.

47. Bureau, circa 1825, Saxony, mahogany, three drawers, flanking columns, gilded bases and capitals, projecting triangular gable. $4,500-6,000. 5,500 E

48. Bureau, circa 1830, Berlin, mahogany, maple, three drawers, flanking columns, triangular gable. 80 cm high, 97 wwide, 51 deep. $7,000-8,000. 7,500 E

49. Bureau, circa 1820, Berlin, mahogany, three drawers, blackened side pilasters, capitals and lion's-paw feet from Berlin foundry, arch segment, inlaid diamond-shaped escutcheons, marble top. 79 cm high, 80 wide, 55 deep. $7,000-8,000. 7,500 E

50

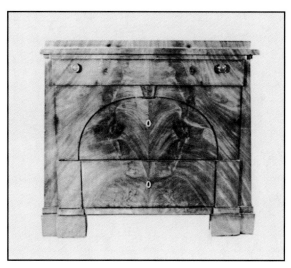

51

50. Bureau, circa 1820, Berlin, walnut, three drawers, projecting lower drawer, arch segment cut into upper drawers, lion heads with rings. 78 cm high, 105 wide, 72 deep. $8,000-9,000. 8,500 E

51. Bureau, circa 1825, Berlin, mahogany, two drawers, slightly conical basic form, drawers overlapping at sides worked as projecting archway design. 84 cm high, 93 wide, 50 deep. $4,500-6,000. 5,000 E

52. Bureau, circa 1825, Berlin, mahogany, three drawers, draws overlapping at sides, with geometrical cutout. $4,000-5,000. 4,500 E

52

53

54

55

53. Bureau, circa 1840, Pomerania, birch, four drawers, stepped bottom and top drawers overlapping sides, front belt with triangular gable, curved bottom panel under British influence. 86 cm high, 87 wide, 48 deep. $2,500-3,500. 3,000 E

54. Bureau, circa 1820, eastern Brandenburg, mahogany, three drawers, projecting bottom drawer with wedge profile, flanking columns. 76 cm high, 86 wide, 54 deep. $4,000-5,000. 4,500 E

55. Bureau, circa 1825, Saxony-Anhalt, ash root, three drawers, projecting bottom drawer with wedge profile, flanking columns. 90 cm high, 100 wide, 55 deep. $7,000-7,500. 7,000 E

56

57

Along with the forms seen in #48-49, a clearly contoured bureau form, usually without columns, is found in the north German areas.

56. Bureau, circa 1825, northern Germany, mahogany, slightly projecting and overlapping bottom drawer. 88 cm high, 86 wide, 54 deep. $3,500-4,000. 4,000 E

57. Bureau, circa 1820, northern Germany, mahogany, two drawers, flanking ebonized columns, choice veneer with flame pattern. 78 cm high, 83 wide, 49 deep. $2,500-3,250. DM, 3,000 E

58. Bureau, circa 1825, northern Germany, mahogany, birch, three drawers, slightly projecting bottom drawer, top drawer with bordered birch panel, middle drawer with arched panel, curved bottom panel in British style, transforming to pointed feet. 83 cm high, 75 wide, 46 deep. $2,500-3,500. 3,000 E

58

59

60

61

59. Bureau, circa 1825, Rhineland, cherry, four drawers, flanking ebonized pillars, gilded bases and capitals, inlaid diamond-shaped escutcheons. 85 cm high, 115 wide, 65 deep. $4,250-5,000. 4,500 E

60. Bureau, circa 1820, Rhineland, ash, three drawers, flanking conical columns, gilded bases and capitals, ebonized edges, inlaid diamond-shaped escutcheons, 86 cm high, 110 wide, 56 deep. $4,500-5,500. 5,000 E

61. Bureau, dated 1803, signed with pencil, made by Albert Hohmann of Elm near Schlüchtern (Hesse), birch, pear, polished black, two drawers, inlaid diamond-shaped escutcheons. 85 cm high, 114 wide, 57 deep. $4,500-5,500. 5,000 E

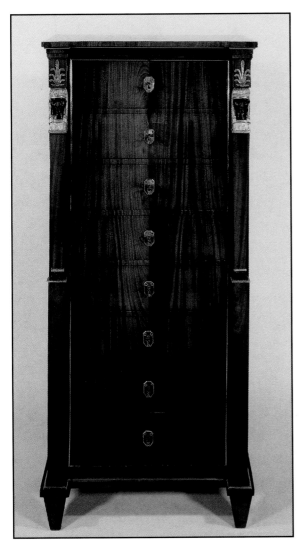

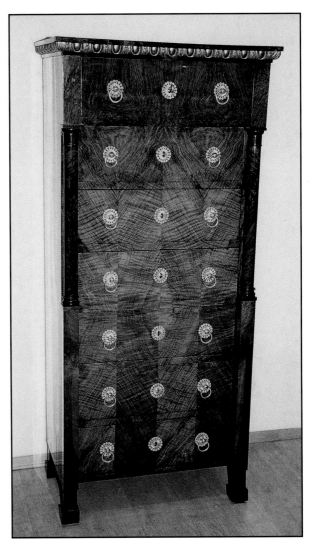

62

63

Pillar bureaus were often placed between windows at "wall pillars."

62. Chiffonier, circa 1815, Vienna, mahogany, bust pilasters above, Egyptian-style caryatids, eight drawers, original brass hardware, brass palmettes, brass border all around. 136 cm high, 51 wide, 36 deep. $11,000-12,000. 11,500 E

63. Chiffonier, circa 1820, Vienna, walnut, seven drawers, three in the middle flanked by inset columns, original fire-gilded hardware, border with ovals above top drawer. 140 cm high, 68 wide, 48 deep. $10,000-11,000. 11,000 E

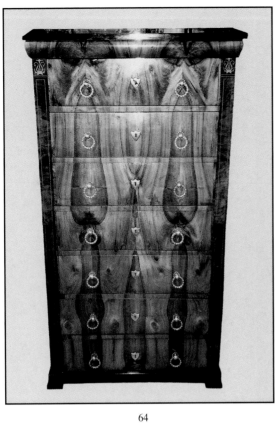

64

66

65

64. Chiffonier, circa 1830, Bohemia, walnut, maple, seven drawers, 150 cm high, 90 wide, 46 deep. $6,000-7,500. 7,000 E

65. Chiffonier, circa 1820, Austria, walnut, seven drawers, inlaid shield-shaped escutcheons. 164 cm high, 60 wide, 42 deep. $6,500-7,500. 7,000 E

66. Chiffonier, circa 1820, Upper Bavaria, cherry, maple, seven drawers, inlaid shield-shaped escutcheons. 140 cm high, 64 wide, 41 deep. $10,000-11,000. 11,000 E

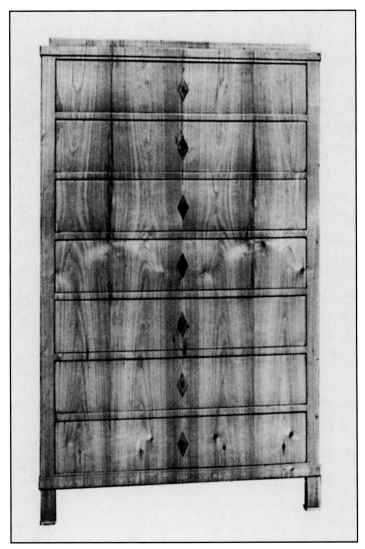

67

68

67. Chiffonier, circa 1825, southern Germany, cherry, seven drawers, inlaid diamond-shaped escutcheons. 155 cm high, 96 wide, 48 deep. $6,000-6,500. 6,500 E

68. Chiffonier, circa 1825, southern Germany, walnut, six drawers, two flanking inset ebonized columns. 140 cm high, 65 wide, 49 deep. $6,500-8,000. 7,000 E

69

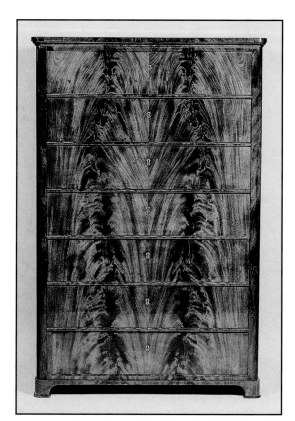

70

71

72

73

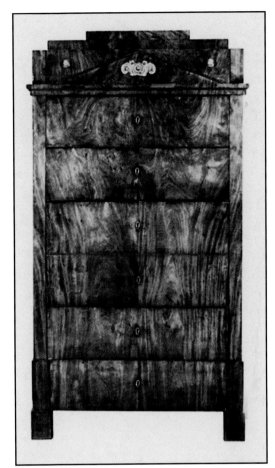

74

69. Chiffonier, circa 1835, Thuringia, cherry, seven drawers, stepped top above top drawer. 167 cm high, 103 wide, 57.5 deep. $13,500-14,500. 14,000 E

70. Chiffonier, circa 1835, probably from Leipzig, seven drawers, Cuban pyramid mahogany, fine S-shaped brass keyholes. 147 cm high, 98 wide, 50 deep. $8,250-9,000. 8,500 E

71. Rear view.

72. Side view.

73. Chiffonier, circa 1820, Brandenburg, mahogany, seven drawers, flanking inset columns with carved capitals and rectangular bases, top with triangular gable and steps. 164 cm high, 107 wide, 59 deep. $6,000-8,000. 7,000 E

74. Chiffonier, circa 1815, northern Germany, mahogany, stepped top set off by top border with projecting gable and fitted drawer plus ornamental bronze hardware, the two middle drawers combined into one drawer. 161 cm high, 90 wide, 49 deep. $8,000-10,000. 9,000 E

75

76

77

75. Sideboard, circa 1820, Austria, walnut, maple inside, two doors, drawer, free side columns, pilasters behind them, rich capitals, gilded oval-pattern border, fire-gilded hardware 100 cm high, 112 wide, 66 deep. $25,000-30,000. 28,500 E

76. Cabinet chest, circa 1810, Vienna, mahogany, floral marquetry, two doors, drawer, flanking carved, partly gilded, partly ebonized bust pilasters, gilded oval-pattern border, reddish marble top, two brass drawer-pulls in lion's-head form, long oval lock shields. 93 cm high, 91 wide, 47 deep. $14,000-15,000. 14,500 E

77. Pair of half-cupboards, circa 1815, Vienna, walnut, two pilasters with antique-style female busts, on conical posts flank the star-pattern arched doors with central bar latch and support the slightly projecting one-drawer top. 155 cm high, 92 wide, 49 deep. $20,000-24,000. 22,500 E

78

79

78. Cabinet chest, circa 1840, Saxony, mahogany, stripe marquetry, two doors, drawer, inlaid shield-shaped escutcheons. 66 cm high, 120 wide, 47 deep. $4,250-4,750. 4,500 E

79. Cabinet chest, circa 1845, Saxony, cherry, doors, drawer. 85 cm high, 80 wide, 40 deep. $3,750-4,250. 4,000 E

80. Cabinet chest, circa 1825, Brandenburg, birch, doors, side columns. 82 cm high, 79 wide, 47 deep. $3,000-3,750. 3,500 E

80

81

82

83

81. Writing cabinet, circa 1835, Austria, walnut, projecting top drawer with folding front and multiple-drawer secretary arrangement, contour edged with rosewood rails, flanking inset ebonized half-columns. 96 cm high, 126 wide, 61 deep. $5,500-6,500. 6,000 E

82. Writing cabinet, circa 1820, Austria, ash, projecting top drawer with folding front and mutliple-drawer secretary arrangement, contour edged with rails, flanking inset ebonized columns. 96 cm high, 125 wide, 62 deep. $5,500-6,500. 6,000 E

83. Writing cabinet, circa 1830, southern Germany, cherry, projecting top drawer with folding front and multiple-drawer secretary arrangement, flanking inset ebonized columns. 97 cm high, 125 wide, 61 deep. $7,000-7,500. 7,500 E

84

85

84. Writing cabinet, circa 1825, southwestern Germany, walnut, projecting top drawer with folding front and mutliple-drawer secretary arrangement, flanking inset ebonized half-columns. 93 cm high, 122 wide, 63 deep. $5,000-6,000. 5,500 E

85. Writing cabinet, circa 1820, southwestern Germany, walnut including crosscut, birch root, maple, projecting top drawer with folding front and four-drawer secretary arrangement, flanking inset ebonized columns, original stamped brass hardware. 95 cm high, 112 wide, 57 deep. $5,500-6,500. 6,000 E

86. Writing cabinet, circa 1835, Thuringia, cherry, projecting top drawer with folding front and two-drawer secretary division, flanking inset ebonized half-columns. 90 cm high, 105 wide, 58 deep. $7,000-8,000. 7,500 E

86

87

90

88

91

89

92

93

94

87. Rolltop secretary, circa 1815, southern Germany, walnut, two drawers, multi-drawer secretary interior, sliding writing panel, cylinder lock, top drawer. 120 cm high, 119 wide, 66 deep. $6,000-7,500. 7,000 E

88. Rolltop secretary, circa 1820, southern Germany, cherry, tw drawers, multi-drawer secretary interior, sliding writing panel, cylinder lock, pierced crown, stamped brass hardware, inlaid diamond-shaped escutcheons. 120 cm high, 128 wide, 59 deep. $6,500-8,000. 7,500 E

89. Rolltop secretary, circa 1815, southern Germany, walnut, two drawers, multi-drawer secretary interior, sliding writing panel, cylinder lock, inlaid escutcheons, 100 cm high, 115 wide, 60 deep. $11,000-12,000. 11,500 E

90. Rolltop secretary, circa 1825, southern Germany, cherry, three drawers, writing panel, multi-drawer secretary interior, stamped brass hardware, three drawers and gallery in top. 136 cm high, 119 wide, 58 deep. $8,500-9,500. 9,000 E

91. Rolltop secretary, circa 1835, northern Germany, mahogany, multi-drawer secretary interior with architectonic middle drawer with steel decor, sliding writing panel with simultaneously opening cylinder lock, two drawers optically joined by arch segment, the upper one with decorative panel set in. 120 cm high, 110 wide, 56 deep. $4,500-5,500. 5,000 E

92. Rolltop secretary, circa 1825, Thuringia, cherry, three drawers, multi-drawer secretary interior, sliding writing panel with simultaneously opening secretary section closed by cylinder lock, flanking inset half-columns, two stepped top drawers, upper one rounded. $5,000-6,000. 5,500 E

93. Folding secretary, circa 1830, southern Germany, walnut, multi-drawer secretary interior, writing panel, side ebonized columns, projecting top drawer. $7,000-$8,000. 7,500 E

94. Folding secretary, circa 1815, Baden, walnut, two drawers, multi-drawer secretary interior, inlaid shield-shaded escutcheons. 113 cm high, 128 wide, 61 deep. $5,000-6,500. 6,000 E

95. Folding secretary, circa 1830, northern Bohemia, oak, two drawers, multi-drawer secretary interior, angled writing panel, stamped brass hardware, triangular segment in top, flanking inset half-columns in bureau part. 150 cm high, 114 wide, 52 deep. $4,000-4,500. 4,500 E

95

97

98

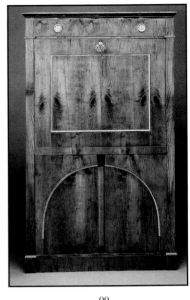

99

96

96. Lady's secretary, dated 1809, signed and stamped Lambert Koch, Vienna, mahogany, two doors below, projecting drawer above them, top drawer and bookshelves in upper part, carved and gilded eagles' heads, caryatids and paws, fire-gilded bronze hardware. 145 cm high, 60 wide, 40 deep. $50,000-60,000. 55,000 E

97. Writing cabinet, circa 1815, Vienna, pear, black polished, maple, cherry, ebonized body, two doors below, writing panel, behind it drawers, three arched compartments, flanking and separating caryatids, top drawer, fire-gilded bronze hardware. 148 cm high, 87 wide, 42 deep. $34,000-39,000. 35,500 E

98-99. Writing cabinet, circa 1815, Vienna, cherry, maple, pear, black polished, two doors and arch segment below, writing panel, drawers behind it around central pigeonhole with arch and triangular gable, lower drawer with wall marquetry, secret compartments, fire-gilded bronze hardware, capitals and bars. 154 cm high, 96 wide, 46 deep. $45,000-50,000. 47,000 E

100

101

103

100. Writing cabinet, circa 1815, Vienna, pear, maple, ash, polished black, ebonized body, two doors below, three drawers behind them, writing panel, multiple drawers behind it, black-lead painting, top drawer, original fire-gilded bronze hardware. 156 cm high, 94 wide, 46 deep. $18,000-19,500. 18,500 E

101. Writing cabinet, circa 1825, Austria, walnut, poplar root, birch root, three drawers below, flanking side columns, writing panel, central tempietto with triple reflection, surrounded by drawers, four columns, black-lead painting on the top and bottom, secret compartments, top drawer, gable-like top, original fire-gilded bronze hardware. 163 cm, 103 wide, 50 deep. $29,000-32,500. 30,000 E

102. Writing cabinet, circa 1815, Vienna, pear, polished black, maple, ebonized body, two doors below, writing panel, painted drawers behind it, secret compartment, top drawer, original fire-gilded bronze hardware. 148 cm high, 90 wide, 42 deep. $19,000-22,500. 21,500 E

103. The same piece closed.

102

104

105

106

107

104. Writing cabinet, circa 1835, Vienna, some crosscut, two doors below, channeled bottom crossbar, flanking ebonized columns with gilded bases and capitals, bottom curves forward slightly, writing panel, multiple drawers behind it, top drawer. $17,500-19,000. 18,500 E

105. The same piece open.

106. Writing cabinet, black shield with black lettering, H. L. Wagner, Vienna, 1837 (Heinrich or Leopold Wagner), walnut, bolt maple, two doors below, three drawers behind them, side three-quarter columns, half-columns channeled backward, writing panel, several drawers behind it, ebonized, reflecting back wall, pilasters on ebonized bases, top drawer projecting slightly, blackened edges, traverses and drawer knobs also ebonized, inlaid ebonized diamond-shaped escutcheons. 156 high, 102 wide, 48 deep. $18,000-19,000. 18,500 E

107. The same piece open.

108

109

A rich interior design with pigeonholes, drawers (some secret drawers), columns and architectural and figured marquetry, increases the value of the piece. The contrast between the wood tones of the body and those of the interior is often deliberate.

108. Writing cabinet, circa 1810, Vienna, walnut, some crosscut, maple, elm, partly ebonized, two drawers below, flanking inset half-columns, writing panel, behind it twelve drawers around a central compartment with mirror in back, top drawer as folding panel, gable curved with three steps, original fire-gilded bronze hardware. 167 cm high, 94 wide, 46 deep. $9,000-11,000. 10,000 E

109. Writing cabinet, circa 1845, Austria, cherry, three drawers below, writing panel, top drawer, molding with cornice profile, flanking inset three-quarter columns. 175 cm high, 103 wide, 48 deep. $7,000-8,500. 8,000 E

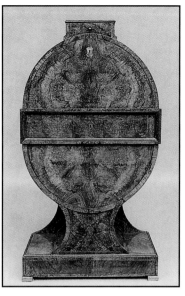

110

111

113

112

110. Lyre secretary, dated 1816, monogrammed J. S. (probably Josef Schwarz), Vienna, walnut including root, maple root, drawers in lower part and foot, writing panel slides out of the oval writing section with folding flap and large upper flap for use as a lectern, several drawers inside, central drawer in upper part flanked by ebonized half-columns, small top drawer. 134 cm high, 72 wide, 35 deep. $50,000-60,000. 55,000 E

111. The same piece closed.

112. Lyre secretary, circa 1830, Austria-Hungary, walnut including crosscut, maple, marquetry, large drawer below, conical middle section with writing panel, lavish interior with drawers, tempietto, pigeonholes, drawer above them, crowned by flat top, inlaid escutcheons. 176 cm high, 102 wide. $65,000-75,000. 70,000 E

113. Lyre secretary, circa 1835, Hungary, mahogany, two drawers below, writing panel, several drawers behind it with spring drawer and secret compartments, profiled top molding extending far out, body curved in below. 155 cm high, 123 wide, 43 deep. $30,000-35,000. 33,000 E

114

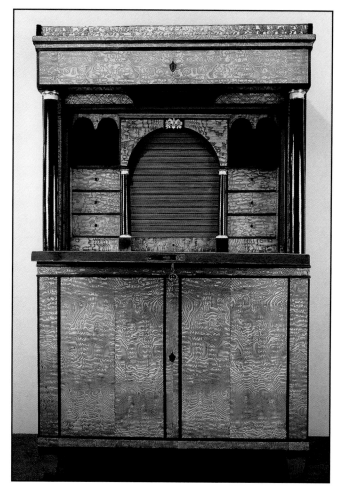

115

Secret compartments: there are secret compartments behind drawers, built-in pieces or columns, as well as with hidden locks. Counter-veneering is supposed to hinder the contraction and cracking of the veneer wood.

114. Writing cabinet, circa 1815, Prague, walnut including crosscut, maple, side stripes and caryatid pilasters with black-lead painting on maple, two doors below, writing panel, lavish interior with secret compartments, three counter-veneered drawers below, original fire-gilded bronze hardware. 147 cm high, 90 wide, 45.5 deep. $27,500-32,500. 30,000 E

115. Writing cabinet, circa 1820, Hungary, flowering ash, elm, boxwood, yew, two doors below, narrow traverse, dark band inlays frame the formative elements, flanking inset ebonized columns with gilded bronze bases and bronze capitals, writing panel with dark band inlays, inside ebonized platform with columns, central compartment closed by shutter, several drawers, inset arch, inlaid pearl-shaped ebonized escutcheons, 144.5 cm high. 89.5 wide, 41.5 deep. $25,000-28,000. 27,000 E

116

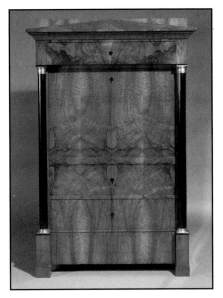

118

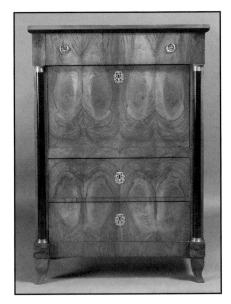

119

117

116. Writing cabinet, circa 1815, Munich, cherry, alder root, maple, two drawers below, flanking ebonized columns, gilded capitals and bases, writing panel, several drawers behind it, very lavish central area with reflections, silver and gold painting, three colored lithographs, ebonized columns, top drawer, lavish architectonically designed top with numerous columns and arches, triangular gable crown. 186 cm high, 97 wide, 53.5 deep. $125,000-140,000. 135,000 E

117. The same piece open.

118. Writing cabinet, circa 1830, southern Germany, walnut including crosscut, maple, birch, flanking ebonized columns on plinth bases, writing panel, six drawers behind it plus architectonically designed pigeonhole with six columns and mirrored back wall, projecting top drawer, molding with triangular gable and stepped top, inlaid diamond-shaped escutcheons, 170 cm high, 115 wide, 56.6 deep. $8,500-10,000. 9,500 E

119. Writing cabinet, circa 1825, southern Germany, walnut including crosscut, cherry, two drawers below, partly colored green, flanking ebonized half-columns, writing panel, central architectonically designed pigeonhole, top drawer, original fire-gilded bronze hardware. 145 cm high, 103 wide, 54 deep. $10,000-13,000. 12,000 E

120

121

122

120. Writing cabinet, circa 1820, Upper Bavaria, cherry, three drawers below, writing panel, ebonized inside—seven drawers behind it, upper drawer slides out as lectern, two small drawers behind it, inlaid shield-shaped escutcheons. $15,000-17,000. 16,000 E

121. The same piece open.

122. Writing cabinet, circa 1820, Upper Bavaria, cherry, two drawers below, writing panel, seven drawers behind it around central pigeonhole, top drawer, inlaid diamond-shaped ebonized escutcheons. 162 cm high, 90 wide, 45 deep. $12,000-14,000. 13,000 E

123. Writing cabinet, signed Joseph Nussbaumer, dated 1826, cherry, three drawers below, flanking ebonized three-quarter columns, writing panel, fourteen drawers behind it, some sharply curved, mirrored compartment with ebonized columns, top drawer, wedge-shaped top design. 160 cm high, 107 wide, 54 deep. $15,000-20,000. 17,500 E

123

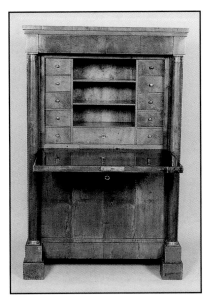

125

126

127

124

124 Writing cabinet, circa 1825, southwestern Germany, walnut including crosscut, two doors below, writing panel, several drawers behind it, flanking ebonized columns, elaborate interior, top drawer with secret compartment, inlaid escutcheons. 151 cm high, 98 wide, 55 deep. $14,000-16,000. 15,000 E

125. Writing cabinet, circa 1825, southwestern Germany, cherry, two doors below, writing panel, eleven drawers and two pigeonholes behind it, top drawer, flanking columns with brass bases and capitals, inlaid brass escutcheons. $12,000-14,000. 13,000 E

126. Writing cabinet, circa 1825, southwestern Germany, walnut, mahogany, birch, three drawers below, flanking ebonized columns, several drawers with architectonically designed mirrored central compartment, top drawer. 145 cm high, 112 wide, 60 deep (in southwestern Germany the veneer pattern was influenced by France). $7,500-10,000. 9,000 E

127. Writing cabinet, circa 1825, southwestern Germany, cherry, three drawers below, flanking ebonized columns, writing panel, drawers and pigeonholes behind it, top drawer. 152 cm high, 103 wide, 52 deep. $7,000-8,500. 8,000 E

128a

129

To obtain unusual veneer patterns, twisted branches and roots of certain types of trees were used.

128. Writing cabinet, circa 1810, eastern Baden, cherry, poplar root, yew, maple, swamp oak, two doors below, flanking ebonized half-columns, writing panel with veneer in various woods, projecting top with integrated drawer, small drawer set above it, several drawers with ebonized veined poplar knobs, central pigeonhole of alder and poplar, inset cherry arcade, inlaid ebonized escutcheons. 164 cm high, 95 wide, 44 deep. $22,500-24,000. 23,000 E

128a. Writing cabinet, circa 1820, Strasbourg, three drawers below, writing panel, drawers and pigeonholes behind it, flanking inset columns with ebonized bases and capitals, top drawer. $13,000-15,000. 14,000 E

129. Writing cabinet, circa 1815, Franconia, elm root, maple, linden, three drawers below, writing panel ebonized inside, flanking ebonized columns with carved and blackened Moors above the gilded capitals, nine drawers inside, pigeonholes with fine marquetry and ebonized columns, drawer in top and two drawers with tendril marquetry above, flanked by two carved and blackened sphinxes. 170 cm high, 92.5 wide, 50 deep. $15,000-19,000. 17,000 E

128

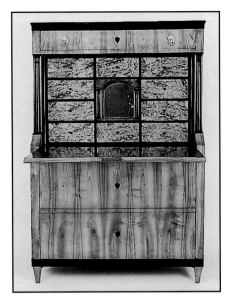

131

132

133

130

130. Writing cabinet, circa 1825, Franconia, cherry, green etched maple, three drawers below, flanked by ebonized half-columns, same above, writing panel ebonized inside, several drawers behind, oval medallion with black-lead painting, four gilded statues of the seasons between pilasters and arches, top drawer, gable of green etched veined root wood, inlaid ebonized shield-shaped escutcheons. 155 cm high, 100 wide, 61 deep. $17,500-20,000. 18,000 E

131. Writing cabinet, circa 1820, Franconia, cherry, two drawers below, ebonized writing panel, flanked by ebonized columns, several drawers, central compartment with arch, columns and marquetry, top drawer, inlaid ebonized shield-shaped escutcheons. 165 cm high, 105 wide, 56 deep $12,000-14,000. 13,000 E

132. Writing cabinet, circa 1825, Franconia, ash, cherry, two drawers below, writing panel, flanked by ebonized vertical stripes, drawers around central compartment with arch and columns, top drawer. 174 cm high, 112 wide, 57 deep. $5,000-6,000. 5,500 E

133. Writing cabinet, dated and signed 1861, Johann Hilpert, Würzburg, three drawers below, writing panel, several drawers inside, central compartment flanked by two ebonized columns. $3,500-4,500. 4,000 E

134

136

137

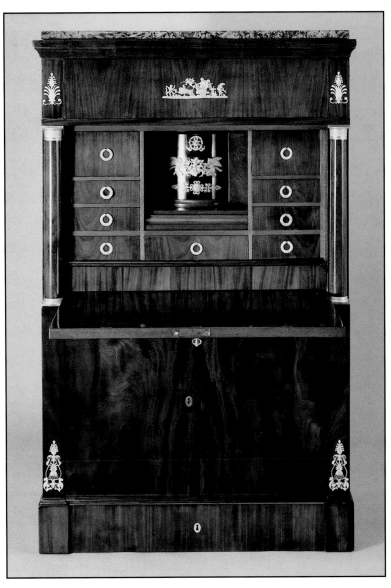

134. Writing cabinet, circa 1810, Thuringia, birch, cherry, ebony, two drawers below, writing panel, flanking caryatid pilasters, several drawers inside, central drawer flanked by two ebonized columns, top drawer, triangular gable with stepped top, fine line inlays, inlaid escutcheons with brass rims. 161 cm high, 99 wide, 54 deep. $11,000-13,000. 12,000 E

135. Writing cabinet, dated July 18, 1818, Rudolstadt, mahogany, poplar root top plate, two doors below, writing panel, several drawers behind it around central compartment, turning cylinder with more drawers, flanking inset columns, top drawer, original fire-gilded bronze hardware. 161 cm high, 93 wide, 60 deep. $45,000-47,500. 47,000 E

136. Writing cabinet, circa 1820, signed Gottlieb Sattler, Neustadt an der Orla under top, cherry, three drawers below, flanking ebonized columns, writing panel, several drawers inside, central compartment flanked by two columns, top drawer, stepped top, inlaid diamond-shaped escutcheons. 160 cm high, 115 wide, 52 deep. $12,000-14,000. 13,000 E

137. Writing cabinet, circa 1825, Thuringia, cherry, three drawers below, flanking ebonized columns, writing panel, several drawers behind it, central compartment with arch, top drawer, inlaid ebonized escutcheons. $14,000-17,500. 16,000 E

135

138   140   141

138. Writing cabinet, circa 1825, Thuringia, walnut, three drawers below, writing panel, several drawers behind it, flanking ebonized columns, top drawer, stepped top. 160 cm high, 110 wide, 54 deep. $17,000-18,000. 17,500 E

139. Writing cabinet, circa 1825, Thuringia, birch, maple, root woods, partly burn-shaded, two drawers below, writing panel, two doors and drawers behind it around central compartment with arch, sunwheel motif, secret compartments, top drawer, stepped top. 165 cm high, 100 wide, 43 deep. $15,000-17,000. 16,000 E

140. Writing cabinet, circa 1830, Thuringia, walnut including crosscut, cherry, maple, two drawers below, flanking ebonized columns with gilded bases and capitals, ebonized writing panel, several drawers behind it, central compartment flanked by two columns, mirror, top drawer, triangular gable in front of steps. 165 cm high, 110 wide, 50 deep. $12,500-14,000. 13,000 E

141. Writing cabinet, Thuringia, label Property of Mathilde C. T. Grabow of Weimar June 1815, apple, plum, root woods, two drawers below, ebonized writing panel, six drawers behind it plus two open compartments around central doors, top drawer, stepped top. 139 cm high, 88 wide, 43 deep. $10,000-12,000. 11,000 E

139

142

144

145

142. Writing cabinet, dated 1817 inside, Thuringia, cherry, birchroot, conically tapering body, three drawers with arch below, writing panel four drawers and pigeonholes behind it, spring mechanism releasing two secret drawers, advanced pilasters, mirror, parquet marquetry, water-color painting, top drawer, ebonized cut-in diamond pattern, triangular gable with toothed frieze and steps, inlaid shield-shaped escutcheons, brass hardware. 161 cm high, 96 wide, 50 high. $12,500-16,000. 15,000 E

143. Writing cabinet, circa 1825, Thuringia, cherry, root woods, three drawers below, writing panel, several drawers behind it around central compartment, top drawer, steps, conical body. $14,000-17,000. 16,000 E

144. Writing cabinet, signed made by journeyman cabinetmaker Friedrich Karl Trautner of Kaulsdorf, 1837, Saalfeld (southern Thuringia) in a secret inside drawer, pear and apple, poplar and ash root, maple, three drawers below, flanking root wood columns, writing panel, eight drawers behind it, two pigeonholes, central compartment with ebonized steps and parquet marquetry, top drawer, central top with arch and ornament, inlaid four-cornered escutcheons. 175 cm high, 105 wide, 55 deep. $11,500-14,000. 13,000 E

145. Writing cabinet, circa 1820, Thuringia, birch, maple, two drawers below, writing panel, drawers behind it around central doors, sun wheel motif, semicircular drawer in top, steps, inlaid diamond-shaped escutcheons. $12,500-14,000. 13,000 E

143

146

148

149

147

146. Writing cabinet, dated 1828, Thuringia, signed by Master Hager, Weimar, pearl, birch, birch root, three drawers below, writing panel, several drawers behind it, middle compartment with triangular gable, top drawer, crown with triangular gable and door, stamped brass hardware. 194 cm high, 112 wide, 52 deep. $7,000-9,000. 8,000 E

147. Writing cabinet, circa 1825, Thuringia, birch, mahogany, maple, swamp oak, three drawers below, flanking inset columns with gilded bases and capitals, writing panel, eight drawers behind it, pigeonhole in portico form with triangular gable, top drawer, crown with triangular gable. 139 cm high, 109 wide, 61 deep. $7,000-9,000. 8,000 E

148. Writing cabinet, circa 1825, northern Thuringia, mahogany, partly ebonized birch root, two drawers below with recessed arcade decor, top drawer, writing panel, several drawers behind it, open central space as portico, step and wall decor, secret compartments. 145 cm high, 112 wide, 53 deep. $7,000-9,000. 8,000 E

149. Writing cabinet, circa 1825, northern Thuringia/Saxony-Anhalt, mahogany, birch, three drawers below with recessed arcade arch, writing panel, several drawers behind it with birch veneer around central space with steps, arch and triangular gable, secret compartment, top drawer, brass hardware and keyhole liners. 144 cm high, 112 wide, 53 deep. $7,500-8,500. 8,000 E

150

151

152

153

150. Writing cabinet, circa 1835, Thuringia, two drawers below, side columns with lavishly carved capitals, writing panel, drawers behind it, top drawer, ornate top above triangular gable. 180 cm high, 110 wide, 60 deep. $17,000-18,000. 17,500 E

151. Writing cabinet, circa 1835, Saxony, reigning house of Anhalt-Dessau, birch, cherry, maple, three drawers below, writing panel, several drawers with inlays behind, arches resting on pillars, top drawer, curved crown, stamped brass hardware. 167 cm high, 100 wide, 52 deep. $13,500-15,000. 14,500 E

152. Writing cabinet, circa 1840, Saxony, cherry, mahogany, maple marquetry, three drawers below, thin flanking double columns, writing panel, several drawers with marquetry behind it, middle space flanked by two columns, top drawer, stepped top with cushion shape on top, four-cornered inlaid escutcheons. 180 cm high, 105 wide, 60 deep. $17,500-19,500. 18,500 E

153. The same piece open.

154

155

156

157

154. Writing cabinet, circa 1832, Saxony, mahogany, maple, birch, three drawers below, flanking inset columns, writing panel, several drawers behind it, central space flanked by columns, triangular gable above columns, inlaid square escutcheons. 220 cm high, 112 wide, 58 deep. $10,000-12,000. 11,000 E

155. Writing cabinet, circa 1825, northern Saxony, mahogany, three drawers below, writing panel, several drawers behind it, arch with columns, top drawer, top with four columns. 183 cm high, 96 wide, 48 deep. $8,000-10,000. 9,000 E

156. Writing cabinet, circa 1825, northern Saxony, mahogany, three drawers below, writing panel, drawers behind it, top with two doors, flanking side columns in upper and lower parts. 200 cm high, 113 wide, 62 deep. $8,000-9,500. 9,000 E

157. Writing cabinet, signed Joh. Friedrich Kettemann von Hall, dated 1828 Halle, walnut, two drawers below, flanking ebonized columns, several drawers around central compartment with arch, triangular gable and wall marquetry, flanking ebonized columns, top drawer, curved architectural top with door and triangular gable. 195 cm high, 110 wide, 65 deep. By the style and technique this is not from Schwäbisch Hall, but from Halle. $15,000-20,000. 17,000 E

158

159

158. Writing cabinet, circa 1825, Saxony-Anhalt, cherry, ash, maple, three drawers below, writing panel, drawers behind it around three pigeonholes, inset columns, signed copperplate in imprint technique after Hiltl. 212 cm high, 110 wide, 57 deep. 25,000-30,000. 27,000 E

159. Writing cabinet, circa 1820, Saxony-Anhalt, walnut, birch root, three drawers below with geometrical recessed fields, writing panel, drawers behind it around central space, top drawer with recessed ebonized diamond and brass hardware, triangular gable, stepped top. 170 cm high, 105 wide, 55 deep. $15,000-16,500. 16,000 E

160

162

163

161

In Berlin the guild monopoly for the production of furniture was abolished as early as 1794.

160. Writing cabinet, circa 1825, Brandenburg, birch, three drawers below, writing panel flanked by inset columns, top drawer, top with curved door, triangular gable between four columns. $14,000-16,000. 15,000 E

161. Writing Cabinet, circa 1825, Brandenburg, cherry, three drawers below writing panel, drawers inside. $16,000-18,000. 17,000 E

162. Writing cabinet, circa 1830, Berlin, birch, three drawers below, writing panel, inset flanking columns, several drawers and arched openings inside, top drawer, top with curved door flanked by two columns, triangular gable. 199.5 cm high, 103 wide, 59 deep. $8,000-9,000. 8,500 E

163. Writing cabinet, circa 1835, Berlin, mahogany, three drawers below, flanking inset columns, writing panel, top drawer, curved door between two scrolls. 212 cm high, 114 wide, 60 deep. $7,500-9,000. 8,500 E

164

165

Gothic-style decorative elements were already used as ornamentation in Britain in the latter half of the 18th century. They appear in Germany particularly between 1795 and 1810 and then even more so from 1840 on.

164. Writing cabinet, circa 1835, Brandenburg, birch, mahogany, three drawers below, writing panel, central door behind it flanked by drawers, top drawer, two doors in top with Gothic-style arches, triangular gable. $9,000-11,000. 10,000 E

165. Writing cabinet, circa 1825, Brandenburg, birch, three drawers below with recessed arched area, flanking inset columns, writing panel, drawers behind it, top drawer, curved door above flanked by two projecting columns, triangular gable, inlaid ebonized shield-shaped escutcheons. 205 cm high, 111 wide, 61 deep. $14,000-15,000. 14,500 E

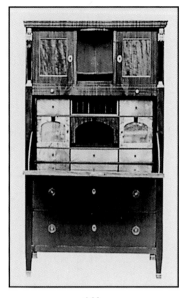

166

168

169

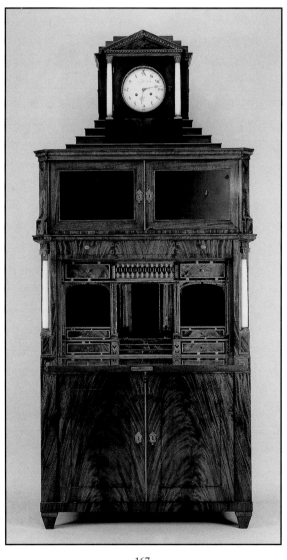

167

166. Writing cabinet, circa 1810, Berlin, mahogany, two drawers below, writing panel, multi-drawer secretary area with pigeonholes, partly with mirrors, sliding tablet panel in stepped edge frieze, two doors in top with mirror niche and flanking caryatid pilasters. 171 cm high, 102 wide, 40 deep. $8,000-10,000. 9,000 E

167. Writing cabinet, circa 1805, Berlin, signed Ruppert, clock signed Kleemeier, mahogany and other wood, two doors below, writing panel flanked by two alabaster columns, several drawers, central pigeonhole with steps, two mirrored doors in upper part, clock above at top of four steps, flanked by two alabaster columns, Arabic numerals, triangular gable. $90,000-110,000. 100,000 E

168. Writing cabinet, circa 1820, Berlin, mahogany, three drawers below, writing panel, flanking columns, top drawer, door in top flanked by two columns, triangular gable. 215 cm high, 110 wide, 55 deep. $8,500-10,000. 9,500 E

169. Writing cabinet, circa 1810, Berlin, mahogany, maple, lemonwood, two drawers below, writing panel, several drawers behind it, top drawer, top with triangular gable, inlaid oval ivory escutcheons. 165 cm high, 95 wide, 40 deep. $14,000-16,000. 15,000 E

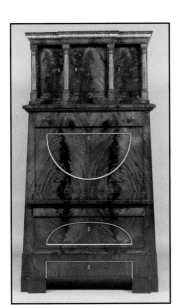

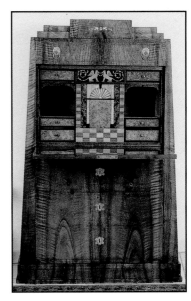

170   171   173

170. Writing cabinet, circa 1820, Berlin, mahogany, conical body, two drawers below, writing panel, several drawers behind it, top drawer, columns and steps in top. 193 cm high, 103 wide, 55 deep. $15,000-17,000. 16,000 E

171. Writing cabinet, circa 1825, Berlin, mahogany, conical body, high base area with hidden drawer, two drawers above it, writing panel, several drawers behind it, top drawer, double-stepped semicircular top, bone knobs, original gilded bronze hardware. 143 cm high, 105 wide, 54.5 deep. $14,000-15,000. 15,000 E

172. Writing cabinet, signed "ce Secretair a été fait par F. A. Voigt Laprit en Decembre 1825, Berlin." Mahogany, three drawers below, flanking inset columns with fire-gilded bronze bases and capitals, writing panel, several drawers behind it, top drawer, stepped triangular gable. 160 cm high, 95 wide, 55 deep. 32,000-34,000. 33,000 E

173. Writing cabinet, circa 1825, southern Brandenburg, signed in pencil on adhesive label Berlin, walnut, maple, mahogany, lemonwood, conical body, three drawers below, writing panel, drawers behind it, two arched niches, central door, marquetry, top drawer, stepped top, original fire-gilded bronze hardware. 158 cm high, 105 wide, 48 deep. $20,000-22,000. 21,000 E

172

174. Writing cabinet, circa 1810, Berlin, mahogany birch root, apple, maple, three drawers below, writing panel with semicircle, flanking pilasters with high-quality marble busts, several drawers inside around pigeonholes, central door, top drawer, cast green iron feet. 147 cm high, 103 wide, 48 deep. $24,000-28,000. 26,000 E

175. Writing cabinet, circa 1845, Lower Saxony, mahogany, maple, marquetry, three drawers below, flanking channeled columns, writing panel, drawers and central niche behind it with columns and triangular gable, top drawer, top above it. $12,500-15,000. 13,500 E

177

178

179

176

176. Lyre secretary, circa 1810, presumably Kassel, mahogany, gilded carvings, two drawers below, writing panel with arch design, secret compartments in a temple-like niche, flanked by several drawers, round section with fan structure in crown, lion's-paw feet, standing on base. 167.5 cm high, 109 wide, 53 deep. $90,000-125,000. 110 E

177. Writing cabinet, circa 1810, eastern Lower Saxony, cherry, two drawers below, writing panel, architectonically designed central door compartment with triangular gable, flanked by pigeonholes mirrored in back, with secret mechanism, top drawer made as angled lectern, central door in top with oval, flanked by two columns. 199 cm high, 105 wide, 48 deep. $9,000-11,000. 10,000 E

178. Writing cabinet, circa 1810, eastern Lower Saxony, probably Braunschweig, birch, birch root, pear, two drawers below, writing panel, drawers behind it, central door above flanked by two alabaster columns and mirrored doors. 198 cm high, 101 wide, 48 deep. $9,000-11,000. 10,000 E

179. Writing cabinet, circa 1810, eastern Lower Saxony, mahogany, two drawers below, writing panel, several drawers behind it, top drawer, stepped top, the elegant middle part with flanking columns and plinth balustrade, oval painted picture with antique-style figures in landscape on the door, side boxes with flat triangular gables, doors with round arched niches. 180 cm high, 90 wide, 45 deep. $9,000-11,000. 10,000 E

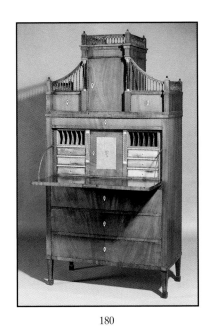

180

181

183

The three-part, clearly stepped top design is typical of northern Germany.

180. Writing cabinet, circa 1810, eastern Lower Saxony, mahogany, maple, three drawers below, writing panel, several drawers and pigeonholes behind it, central door flanked by pilasters, top drawer, central door in top flanked by two columns on bases and two drawers, pierced gallery railing. $8,000-9,000. 8,500 E

181. Writing cabinet, circa 1815, eastern Lower Saxony, in style of Christian Simon, cherry, pear, birch root, walnut, ebony, maple, partly burned, two drawers below, writing panel, thirteen offset drawers around central mirrored door compartment, two pigeonholes with secret drawers above them, two flanking alabaster columns, top drawer tips as lectern, mirrored door in top flanked by alabaster half-columns, small side drawers, multi-stepped wreath profile with crowning pierced gallery. 198 cm high, 95 wide, 47 deep (Compare master design by Christian Simon, March 13, 1815). $10,000-12,000. 11,000 E

182. Writing cabinet, circa 1815, eastern Lower Saxony, cherry, two drawers below, writing panel, drawers behind it, open spaces with galleries, top drawer, central door with oval in top, flanked by two columns with bases and two small drawers, pierced gallery. $12,000-14,000. 13,000 E

183. Writing cabinet, dated 1841, masterpiece by Johann Friedrich Eickhoff, Bremen, mahogany, three drawers below, writing panel, several drawers behind it, central compartment flanked by two columns, top drawer, curved middle door in top flanked by two columns. $10,000-12,000. 11,000 E

182

184

186

187

185

184. Writing cabinet, circa 1820, Braunschweig, mahogany, three drawers below, writing panel, several drawers and pigeonholes behind it, central space flanked by two columns, upper drawer, tempietto with four columns in top, flanked by two doors. 177 cm high, 108 wide, 55 deep. $16,000-18,000. 17,000 E

185 Writing Cabinet, circa 1825, northern Germany, mahogany, three drawers below, writing panel, six drawers behind it, three drawers in upper part, stepped top, inlaid diamond-shaped lock shields. 153 cm high, 104 wide, 50 deep. $7,500-9,000. 8,500 E

186. Lyre secretary, Frankfurt, signed Friedrich Marschall, Master, 1832 in Frankfurt, mahogany veneer on oak, maple, root wood, body curves inward below, drawer, writing panel above, very elegant interior with drawers, four white columns and arch elements, triangular gable in central niche, steps and parquet marquetry, many iron mechanisms for secret and spring drawers, large drawer above made as lectern with further drawer division, multi-stepped top. 165 cm high, 104 wide, 52 deep. $90,000-110,000. 100,000 E

187. The same piece open.

188

190

191

188. Writing cabinet, Frankfurt, signed under the top Conrad Ellerbusch, born in Bremen, made this secretary in Frankfurt on the Main at Master Cabinetmaker Hirt's in 1821, cherry, two drawers below, flanking ebonized columns, writing panel, drawer and space divided by columns behind it, top drawer, capitals, stamped brass, original brass hardware. 159 cm high, 105 wide, 54.5 deep. $19,000-20,000. 19,500 E

189. Writing cabinet, circa 1825, Palatinate, walnut, some crosscut, rosewood, maple, multi-curved bottom apron flanked by two channeled columns, two half-columns behind, writing panel, drawer with brick marquetry behind it, central compartment with mirror flanked by two columns, seven secret drawers, all drawers with hidden knobs and spring power, top drawer, keyholes in French fashion, original fire-gilded hardware. 132 cm high, 92 wide, 49 deep. $40,000-50,000. 45,000 E

190. Writing cabinet, circa 1825, Mainz, walnut, maple, mahogany, three drawers below, writing panel, several drawers behind it, central compartment with mirror, flanked by two white half-columns, flanking half-columns behind, white quarter-columns outside, arch and column structure, projecting top border with top drawer in architrave, removable top, secret compartment under it. 160 cm high, 109 wide, 58 deep. $17,500-$20,000. 19,000 E

191. Writing cabinet, circa 1845, Hesse, cherry, mahogany, two doors below, writing panel, several drawers with inlaid stripes behind it, top drawer. 167 cm high, 100 wide, 52 deep. $9,000-10,000. 10,000 E

189

192

193

By oiling, burning, etching, coloring and polishing the wood grain is enhanced. Etching is generally visible only in places where minimal light falls.

192. Writing cabinet, circa 1825, Rhineland, cherry, mahogany, ash, three drawers below, bottom crossbar curved forward to join with a reversed molding, curved cutout edge on the front, writing panel, two side rows of two drawers each inside, columned portico in the middle with steps and arcade, stepped top with triangular gable. 162.5 cm high, 104.5 wide, 54.5 deep. $15,000-17,500. 16,500 E

193. Writing cabinet, circa 1830, Rhineland, walnut, two drawers below, writing panel, center archway with mirror, top drawer, inlaid shield-shaped brass escutcheons, very lovely veneer pattern throughout. 146 cm high, 103 wide, 50 deep. $9,000-10,000. 9,500 E

194

196

194. Writing cabinet, circa 1815, Rhineland, cherry, two doors below, writing panel, three drawers behind it, archway with eight pillars, maple cube marquetry at the bottom, gilded bases and capitals, top drawer, flanking vertical stripes, greenish-black lion paws, original mahogany-colored polish. $17,500-19,000. 18,000 E

195. Writing cabinet, circa 1830, Rhineland, walnut, three drawers below, writing panel, drawers behind it, top drawer. $13,000-14,000. 13,500 E

196. Writing cabinet, circa 1815, Palatinate, walnut, three drawers below, writing panel, drawers around central compartment, flanked by two columns and two inset ebonized columns, interior with polychrome landscape and scenic painting, Classicistic frieze on the top drawer. $18,000-20,000. 19,000 E

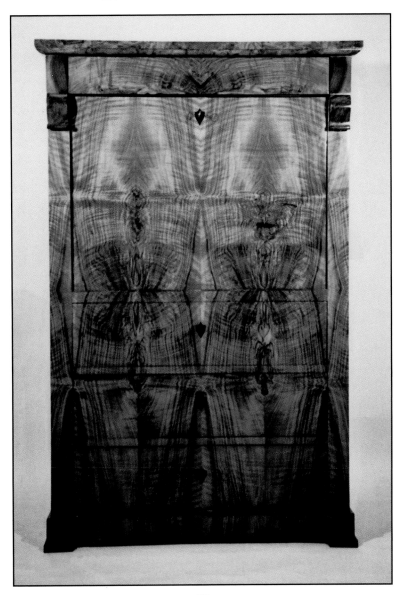

195

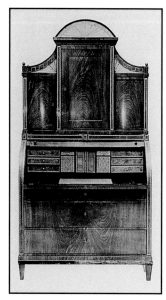

197   198

199

Sea-shell and star-shaped ornaments were very popular in Britain and were taken over in the process of adapting the British styles. Bracket feet are wooden feet with straight outside edges and extended insides.

197. Roll-top secretary, circa 1815, northern Germany, mahogany, three drawers below, roll-top, drawers and pigeonholes behind it, stepped two-door top with straight central section and convex side boxes, crowned with sea-shell marquetry and meander stripe, 228 cm high, 110 wide, 58 deep. $8,000-10,000. 9,000 E

198. Roll-top secretary, circa 1825, northern Germany, mahogany, three drawers below, roll-top, drawer and doors behind it, three doors and drawer in top, so-called bracket feet under British influence. 204 cm high, 120 wide, 53 deep. $7,000-8,500. 8,000 E

199. Roll-top secretary, circa 1825, northern Germany, mahogany, four drawers below, roll-top, drawer and secret compartments behind it, stepped top with marquetry, central section divided into cubicles and folding as lectern, so-called bracket feet. 228 cm high, 128 wide, 66 deep. $6,500-8,500. 7,500 E

200

201

The secretary with an ornate top lost more and more significance since the 19th century began and was replaced more and more by the popular writing cabinet (*Secrétaire á abattant*). Even so, significant examples were still built, mostly with a quarter-round roll-top to cover the writing area, or with a rolling jalousie blind. The angled writing panel in the 18th-century tradition was retained longer in rural areas.

200. Roll-top secretary, circa 1815, northern Germany, mahogany, three drawers enclosed by right and left doors below, jalousie blind, drawers, pigeonholes and central door behind it, jalousie blind in the top between two flanking doors, drawers and pigeonholes behind it, meander stripe at the top. 159 cm high, 117 wide, 74 deep. $8,000-10,000. 9,000 E

201. Roll-top secretary, circa 1840, northern Germany, mahogany, nine drawers below around the open kneehole which has two doors, jalousie blind, two doors in the top, sliding lectern, secret compartments, triangular gable in the middle. 217 cm high, 132 wide, 94.5 deep. $7,000-9,000. 8,000 E

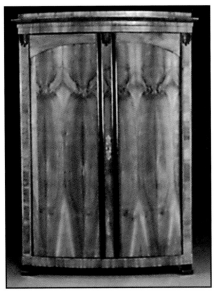

202

203

204

205

202. Cupboard, circa 1830, Vienna, walnut, partly ebonized, two doors, front slightly curved, recessed arch on doors, stepped border. 201 cm high, 146 wide, 55 deep. $7,000-9,000. 8,000 E

203. Cupboard, circa 1830, Vienna, walnut, partly ebonized, two doors with recessed arch. 200 cm high, 136 wide, 56 deep. $12,000-13,500. 13,000 E

204. Cupboard, circa 1835, Austria, walnut, two doors, curved front, flanking channeled columns, recessed arches on doors, inlaid mother-of-pearl escutcheons surrounded by band of ebony. 182 cm high, 116 wide, 58 deep. $6,500-7,500. 7,000 E

205. Cupboard, circa 1825, Austria, walnut, two curved doors with recessed arches, ebonized inset columns, crown molding. $12,500-13,500. 13,000 E

207

208

206. Cupboard, circa 1825, Austria, cherry, two doors, transversely veneered bottom, flanking half-columns, slightly projecting edge, inlaid shield-shaped ebonized escutcheons, projecting top edge. 193 cm high, 137 wide, 59 deep. $11,000-12,000. 12,000 E

207. Cupboard, circa 1830, Austria, walnut, two doors flanked by channeled columns, crown molding with profiled cornice. 193 cm high, 142 wide, 67 deep. $6,500-7,500. 7,000 E

208. Cupboard, circa 1830, Bohemia, walnut, two doors, curved stripes and bottom, top with profiled molding. 190 cm high, 145 wide, 62 deep. $4,000-4,500. 4,500 E

206

209

210

209. Cupboard, circa 1835, Bohemia, walnut, two doors, crown molding, inlaid shield-shaped escutcheons. 195 cm high, 137 wide, 61 deep. $4,500-5,500. 5,000 E

210. Cupboard, circa 1830, Bohemia, walnut, two doors, flanking inset columns with veneer around them, crown molding with profiled cornice, body slightly projecting, 204 cm high. 128 wide, 58 deep. $12,000-13,500. 13,000 E

211   212

211. Cupboard, circa 1815, Austria, walnut veneered and massive, two doors, black-lead painting in upper panels, flanking inset caryatids with Egyptian heads, crown molding. 194 cm high, 140 wide, 57 deep. $15,000-17,000. 16,000 E

212. Cupboard, circa 1820, Austria, walnut, two curving doors, flanking ebonized columns with gilded bases and capitals, ebonized bottom and top molding. $10,000-11,500. 11,000 E

213

215

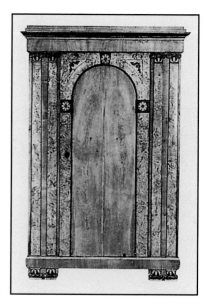

216

214

213. Cupboard, circa 1830, Bohemia, walnut including crosscut, two doors, curved front, flanking diagonally veneered columns and bottom, cornice. 220 cm high, 170 wide, 70 deep. $15,000-17,500. 16,000 E

214. Cupboard, circa 1830, Austria, walnut, two doors, corved front, six channeled columns, ebonized bottom bar, profiled cornice. 198 cm high, 176 wide, 75 deep. $19,000-21,5000. 20,000 E

215. Cupboard, circa 1835, Prague, birch root, doors with two stripe inlays, central lock with iron bar, rounded top plate. 180 cm high, 85 wide, 48 deep. $6,000-7,000. 6,500 E

216. Cupboard, circa 1835, Hungary, cherry, ash root, two wide striped fields with double root wood pilasters flanking the doorframes with rounded arch pattern, top cornices. 180 cm high, 125 wide, 55 deep. $7,000-9,000. 8,000 E

Opposed veneering was supposed to hinder the shrinking and cracking of the veneer.

217. Library cupboard, circa 1825, Austria-Hungary, maple, maple root, knotty maple, mahogany, four doors with maple opposed veneer, top molding, ebonized stripe inlays. 178 cm high, 233 wide, 58 deep. $19,000-21,500. 20,000 E

218. Half-cupboard, circa 1810, Vienna, black lacquered body, one door, flanking inset pilasters with busts, original fire-gilded bronze hardware. 152 cm high, 65 wide, 38 deep. $13,500-14,500. 14,000 E

219. Cupboard, circa 1825, Vienna, mahogany, maple, stripe inlays, two doors, top molding, inlaid diamond-shaped escutcheons, 168 cm high, 87 wide, 36 deep. $18,000-5,000. 5,000 E

218

219

217

221

222

223

220

220. Cupboard, circa 1805, Munich, cherry, elm root, maple, plum, pear, two doors, geometrical marquetry, two angels in black-lead painting on lower parts of doors, flanking ebonized quarter-columns, root wood bottom bar, triangular gable with lavish black-lead painting. A comparable cupboard is in the Munich City Museum. 204 cm high, 165 wide, 67 deep. $140,000-150,000. 145 E

221. Cupboard, circa 1825, southern Germany, cherry, two doors, flanking ebonized columns, ebonized top and bottom bars, cornice. $8,500-10,000. 9,500 E

222. Cupboard, circa 1825, eastern Bavaria, cherry, two doors, flanking ebonized columns, ebonized top and bottom bars, cornice. 190 cm high, 142 wide, 60 deep. $7,000-8,500. 8,000 E

223. Cupboard, circa 1825, southern Germany, cherry, two doors, flanking ebonized columns, ebonized bottom bar, cornice, 202 cm high, 160 wide, 58 deep. $7,500-9,500. 9,000 E

225

227

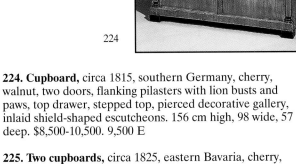

224

224. Cupboard, circa 1815, southern Germany, cherry, walnut, two doors, flanking pilasters with lion busts and paws, top drawer, stepped top, pierced decorative gallery, inlaid shield-shaped escutcheons. 156 cm high, 98 wide, 57 deep. $8,500-10,500. 9,500 E

225. Two cupboards, circa 1825, eastern Bavaria, cherry, two doors, brass hardware. 198 cm high, 134 wide, 60 deep. Pair $10,000-12,500. 11,000 E

226. Cupboard, dated 1838, eastern Bavaria, ash, two doors with panels, flanking side columns, triangular gable, ebonized knobs on top. 212 cm high, 139.5 wide, 62.5 deep. $12,500-13,500. 13,000 E

227. Cupboard, circa 1830, southern Germany, cherry, birch root, two doors, flanking ebonized columns with gilded carved capitals, black top bar, inlaid shield-shaped escutcheons, cornice. 239 cm high, 190 wide, 78 deep. $7,500-10,500. 9,000 E

226

228

229

230

231

228. Cupboard, circa 1820, probably from Simbach on the Inn, walnut, two doors, ebonized bottom bar and pilasters, top molding, pierced top railing, 213 cm high, 144 wide, 60 deep. $12,000-13,500. 13,000 E

229. Cupboard, circa 1830, southern Germany, cherry, two doors with panels, ebonized bottom bar, top molding, stamped brass hardware. $6,000-7,500. 7,000 E

230. Cupboard, circa 1830, southern Germany, cherry, massive, two doors with panels, drawer below, flanking ebonized columns and bottom bar, cornice molding. 199 cm high, 141 wide, 59 deep. $6,500-8,000. 7,500 E

231. Cupboard, circa 1825, Upper Bavaria, cherry, two doors with panels, ebonized bottom bar, partly ebonized grooved molding. 208 cm high, 175 wide, 62 deep. $14,000-16,000. 15,000 E

232

234

235

232. Cupboard, circa 1815, presumably from Stuttgart, cherry, massive and veneered, two doors with panels, angled prismatic pilasters, grooved molding, original brass hardware. 221 cm high, 177.5 wide, 59 deep. $9,000-10,000. 9,500 E

233. Cupboard, circa 1820, Upper Swabia, probably from Biberach, pear, two doors with panels, flanking ebonized half-columns, ebonized bottom bar, grooved profile, raised triangular gable. 212 cm high, 186 wide, 60 deep. $24,000-26,000. 25,000 E

234. Cupboard, circa 1825, Upper Swabia-Eastern Baden, cherry, two doors with panels, tapered sides, top molding. 204 cm high, 176 wide, 57 deep. $8,000-9,000. 8,500 E

235. Cupboard, signed "Margaretha Fuchs von Lachen 1838" (east of Memmingen) inside, floral wreath signed "Alois Widman." Walnut, two doors, flanking ebonized half-columns, grooved molding, stepped base. $7,500-8,500. 8,000 E

233

237

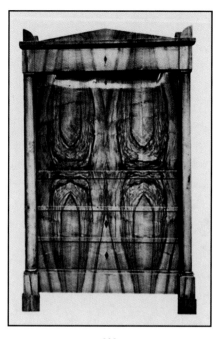

238

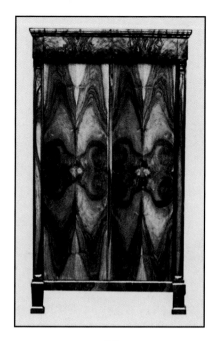

239

236

236. Cupboard, circa 1815, Stuttgart, mahogany, two doors with panels, stepped top with central drawer, cast bronze hardware. 229 cm high, 139 wide, 52 deep. 6,000-8,000. 7,000 E

237. Cupboard, circa 1815, Stuttgart, mahogany, two doors with panels, stepped top with central drawer. 230 cm high, 140 wide, 52 deep. $6,000-8,000. 7,000 E

238. Cupboard, circa 1825, Baden, walnut, front pattern like a writing cabinet, one door. 175 cm high, 113 wide, 59 deep. $4,250-4,500. 4,500 E

239. Cupboard, circa 1830, northern Baden, walnut, two doors, top drawer, triangular molding, flanking inset half-columns, top molding. 181 cm high, 108 wide, 53 deep. $5,000-6,000. 5,500 E

240

241

In Baden in particular, as already in the 18th century, there was a strong French influence. This is shown in the three-section pattern of the panels, the choice of veneer, and often in the lock and bolt system.

240. Cupboard, circa 1835, Baden, cherry, two doors with panels, top molding with rounded corners, inlaid diamond-shaped ebonized escutcheons. 230 cm high, 170 wide, 58 deep. $16,500-18,500. 17,500 E

241. Cupboard, circa 1825, southern Baden, cherry, walnut, maple, two doors curving forward with panels, flanking inset columns, molding with curved cornices, triangular gable. 203 cm high, 158 wide, 64 deep. $8,000-10,000. 9,000 E

243

244

245

242

242. Cupboard, circa 1820, Nuremberg, Pharmacist Billing's family, walnut, two doors with rounded panels, flanking ebonized half-columns, ebonized bottom plate, double head with triangular gable, ebonized toothed pattern. Top, 297 cm high, 155 wide, 62 deep. $15,000-17,500. 16,000 E

243. Cupboard, circa 1820, Franconia, oak, plum, two doors with panels, partly with marquetry, flanking ebonized columns over profiled molding, triangular gable, vases on sides. $11,000-13,000. 12,000 E

244. Cupboard, dated 1826 on lock and monogrammed, Franconia, cherry, two doors with panels, symmetrical veneer, triangular gable over profiled molding. 199 cm high, 143 wide, 58 deep. $13,500-15,000. 14,000 E

245. Cupboard, circa 1825, Franconia, walnut, two doors with panels, flanking ebonized columns and bottom bar, triangular gable over cornice frieze. 225 cm high, 140 wide, 62 deep. $14,000-15,000. 14,500 E

246

247

246. Cupboard, circa 1825, southern Thuringia, cherry, two doors, flanking ebonized side-inset columns, cornice molding. 186 cm high, 128 wide, 55 deep. $9,000-10,000. 9,500 E

247. Cupboard, circa 1825, Palatinate, cherry, two doors, ebonized bottom bar, flanking half-columns on half-round pedestals, ebonized bases and capitals, two panels in sidewalls, triangular gable, ebonized vases on rounded pedestals at the sides, partly ebonized cornice molding, brass hardware. 220 cm high, 155 wide, 62 deep. $11,000-12,500. 12,000 E

248

250

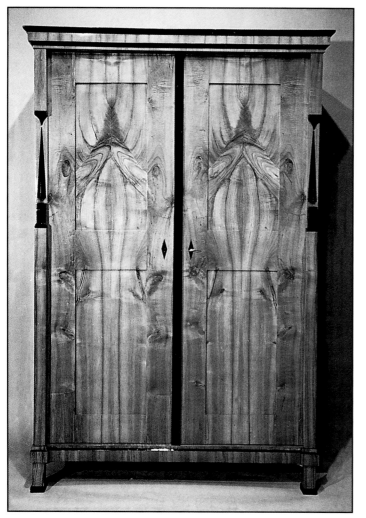

249

248. Cupboard, circa 1825, Hesse, cherry, two doors, stepped top with triangular gable, 198 cm high, 159 wide, 63 deep. $5,500-7,000. 6,000 E

249. Cupboard, circa 1830, Thuringia, two doors, flanking ebonized pyramids and bottom bar, cornice molding, inlaid diamond-shaped lock shields. $10,000-12,500. 12,000 E

250. Cupboard, circa 1825, southeast Thuringia, cherry, two projecting doors in Austrian style, flanking ebonized columns and bottom bar, ebonized triangular segment, stepped top molding. $5,500-7,000. 6,000 E

251

252

253

Rounded corners and curving friezes identify the time of production as after 1835.

251. Cupboard, circa 1850, Hesse, walnut, two doors, ebonized decorative profile. 210 cm high, 152 wide, 55 deep. $2,500-3,250. 3,000 E

252. Cupboard, circa 1815, Thuringia, walnut veneer and oak, two doors, flanking ebonized columns and bottom bar, triangle segment, toothed top molding. 209 cm high, 163 wide, 58 deep. $10,000-12,000. 11,000 E

253. Cupboard, circa 1820, Thuringia, cherry, two doors, inlaid diamond, flower and fan motifs, triangular gable. 200 cm high, 145 wide, 58 deep. $7,500-8,500. 8,000 E

254

256

257

255

254. Cupboard, circa 1835, Rhineland, veneered and massive cherry, two doors, two drawers under them, cornice molding, inlaid pyramid-shaped escutcheons. $17,500-19,000. 18,000 E

255. Cupboard, circa 1835, Rhineland, veneered and massive cherry, two doors with pointed-arch panels, two drawers under them, cornice molding, inlaid ebonized shield-shaped escutcheons. 240 cm high, 187 wide, 76 deep. $19,000-21,000. 20,000 E

256. Cupboard, circa 1820, Westphalia, massive and veneered cherry, ebony intarsia, oak frame, two drawers below, cornice molding, inlaid ebonized square escutcheons, stamped brass appliqués on the pilasters, 208 cm high, 201 wide, 73 deep. $19,000-21,000. 20,000 E

257. Cupboard, circa 1825, Rhineland, cherry, cherry root, two doors, drawer in base with quarter-round form, flanking inset columns, top molding. 228 cm high, 197 wide, 70 deep. $9,000-11,000. 9,500 E

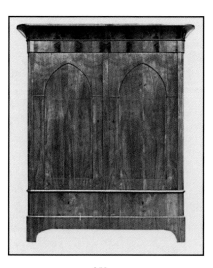

258

259

260

258. Cupboard, circa 1845, Rhineland, cherry, two doors with pointed-arch panels, sharply raked cornice molding with rounded corners. 249 cm high, 208 wide, 83 deep. $7,000-9,000. 8,000 E

259. Cupboard, circa 1840, Rhineland, cherry, two doors with pointed-arch panels, four drawers, cornice molding with rounded corners. $11,500-12,500. 12,000 E

260. Cupboard, circa 1835, Rhineland, cherry, two doors, two bottom drawers, inlaid shield-shaped escutcheons, top molding. $10,000-12,000. 11,000 E

261. Cupboard, circa 1825, Rhineland, cherry, two doors with rounded-arch panels, flanking ebonized columns, two bottom drawers, cornice molding, inlaid diamond-shaped escutcheons. 240 cm high, 180 wide, 70 deep. $23,500-25,000. 24,000 E

261

263

264

265

262

262. Cupboard, circa 1820, Rhineland, cherry, two doors with panels, flanking ebonized columns, bottom bar stays in place when doors are opened, 211 cm high, 165 wide, 64.5 deep. $14,500-16,000. 15,000 E

263. Cupboard, circa 1825, Saxony-Anhalt, mahogany, door with writing-cabinet interior, top molding with ebonized cyma curves. 177 cm high, 116.3 wide, 57.5 deep. $7,500-8,500. 8,000 E

264. Cupboard, circa 1830, Thuringia, walnut, door with writing-cabinet interior, flanking inset columns with bronze bases and capitals, triangular gable, two-stepped top with drawer, toothed molding, compartments inside, inlaid bone escutcheons. 180 cm high, 130 wide, 62 deep. $8,000-9,000. 8.500 E

265. Cupboard, circa 1825, Berlin, birch root, door with writing-cabinet interior, flanking inset columns, triangular gable with toothed molding, stepped crown. 198 cm high, 128 wide, 75 deep. $6,000-7,000. 6,500 E

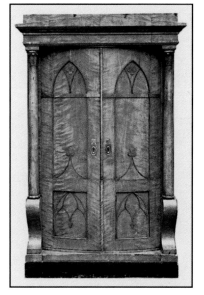

266   267

The often limited living space made it necessary to locate clothing and linen cupboards in living and reception rooms, but they were not to be recognized as such instantly. Thus there arose the so-called "blinder" with writing-cabinet interior, often as a satellite to a writing cabinet.

266. Cupboard, dated 1841, signed on the right side of the top, made by journeyman cabinetmaker August Tankowitz of Danzig at Master Cabinetmaker Kroll's in Burg, door with writing-cabinet interior, flanking half-columns linked to the body with waves, multi-curved top frieze and molding, inlaid escutcheons. $4,500-6,000. 5,000 E

267. Cupboard, circa 1835, Brandenburg, birch, two curved doors with Gothic pointed-arch panels, flanking inset columns on scrolls, Gothic designs with flowers, triangular gable, stepped top. 173 cm high, 117 wide, 66 deep. $6,000-7,000. 6,500 E

268. Cupboard, circa 1825, Brandenburg, birch and birch root, two doors with panels, ebonized bottom bar and inlaid escutcheons, gable with triangular central crown. 238 cm high, 176 wide, 56 deep. $10,000-12,000. 11,000 E

268

270

271

269

269. Cupboard, circa 1815, Saxony-Anhalt, cherry, two doors, green and brown diamond shapes and flowers made of apple wood and flowering ash, two bottom drawers. 218 cm high, 179 wide, 62 deep. $12,000-13,500. 13,000 E

270. Cupboard, circa 1815, northern Germany, mahogany, two doors, bottom with drawer, flanking pilasters, three-stepped cornice molding. 214 cm high, 162 wide, 65 deep. $7,000-8,500. 8,000 E

271. Cupboard, circa 1825, northern Germany, cherry, maple, two doors, flanking inset columns, black-framed panels with parquetry and shell marquetry, also on the bottom, central rosettes on the doors, triangular gable with flanking cornices. 208 cm high, 196.5 wide, 82 deep. $8,000-10,000. 9,000 E

272

273

North German cupboards usually have oak frames.

272. Cupboard, circa 1835, Schleswig-Holstein, oak, maple, root wood, walnut, two doors with greenish-black diamond panel marquetry and antique-style feminine figures, flowers, bird in basket, shell ornament, bottom drawer, body rounded at the edges, triangular gable. 230 cm high, 165 wide, 62 deep. $7,000-9,000. 8,000 E

273. Cupboard, circa 1820, northern Germany, mahogany, two doors, flanking pilasters, bottom drawer, triangular gable. 238 cm high, 197 wide, 70 deep. $7,000-9,000. 8,000 E

274. Cupboard, circa 1810, Eutin, owned by painter Johann Heinrich Wilhelm Tischbein, ash on oak, two doors, bottom bar in pilaster form, two bottom drawers, triangular gable with Doric style elements, inlaid diamond-shaped escutcheons. 250 cm high, 189 wide, 61 deep. $11,000-12,000. 11,500 E

274

276

277

275

275. Bookcase, circa 1820, Vienna, cherry, two doors, upper third glassed with ebonized lyre decoration, middle third has black-lead paintings of landscapes in ovals, flanking ebonized columns, cornice molding. 215 cm high, 160 wide, 56 deep. $31,500-34,000. 33,000 E

276. Bookcase, circa 1815, Vienna, mahogany, maple, stripes at sides, two doors, glassed arches above, gilded profile with ebonized branching pillars, rectangular panels below, cornice molding with gilded oval staff, original brass hardware, maple counter-veneering. 189 cm high, 131 wide, 44 deep. $15,000-17,000. 16,000 E

277. Bookcase, circa 1825, Vienna, flowering ash, two doors glassed above with branched pillars in round arches, rectangular panels below, cornice molding. 186 cm high, 136 wide, 44 deep. $20,000-22,500. 21,000 E

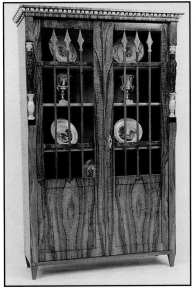

279   280

278. Bookcase, Vienna, signed Albrecht 1825, receipt of Erstes Wiener Möbelheim I, cherry, two doors, glazed above, round arches with many bars, rectangular panels below, cornice molding. 245 cm high, 164 wide, 48.6 deep. $27,500-30,000. 29,000 E

279. Bookcase, circa 1815, Vienna walnut, two doors above with spear bars, flanking gilded carved caryatids, cornice molding with gilded oval staff. 176 cm high, 106 wide, 40 deep. $19,000-21,000. 20,000 E

280. Bookcase, circa 1835, Bohemia, cherry, two doors, glazed above, rectangular panels below, diagonally veneered arched pilasters, cornice molding. $6,000-7,500. 7,000 E

278

281

282

In showcases and bookcases, original glass plates add to the value. They show characteristic flaws and irregularities. The plates were usually puttied inside.

281. Showcase, circa 1830, Vienna, mahogany, maple, stripe decoration, glazed on three sides with branching bars and three gothic-style pointed arches, door complete, triangular gable with set-back top, three sections, mirrored back wall, inlaid decorative capitals. 170 cm high, 118 wide, 48 deep. $15,000-16,000. 15,500 E

282. Showcase, circa 1830, Vienna, cherry, maple, glazed on three sides with branching bars, single door with three Gothic-style pointed arches, triangular gable with set-back top, three sections, original rear mirror and glass, inlaid decorative capitals, very good original condition. 171 cm high, 110 wide, 44 deep, identical model in Austrian Museum of Applied Art. $27,500-32,000. 30,000 E

283

284

A showcase is a container glazed on three or all four sides, while a bookcase, which can also hold dishes, collections or souvenirs, is glazed in the front.

283. Showcase, circa 1830, Vienna, flowering ash, maple, root wood, glazed with branched bars on three sides, one door, set-back top, three sections, inlaid decorative capitals. $19,000-20,000. 19,500 E

284. Showcase, circa 1835, Austria, walnut including crosscut, maple, glazed on three sides, one door, two shelves and two added steps, partly resting on four columns, flanking inset half-columns, quarter-columns in back, cornice molding, bottom drawer. 163 cm high, 76 wide, 44 deep. $5,500-7,000. 6,000 E

285

286

288

287

285. Showcase, circa 1825, Austria, walnut, two doors glazed in oval pattern with ebonized concentric spokes, side pilasters with ball capitals, cornice molding. 94 cm high, 73 wide, 51 deep. $11,000-12,000. 11,500 E

286. Showcase on chest, circa 1825, Vienna, cherry, two-doored upper part with partly ebonized molding, glazed doors with geometrical bar pattern, ebonized diamond lines, inlaid brass lock shields. 219 cm high, 136 wide, 55 deep. $17,500-19,000. 18,500 E

287. Bookcase, circa 1835, Austria, walnut, three glazed doors with ebonized pointed-arch bar patterns, channeled pilasters, panels below, cornice molding. 198 cm high, 203 wide, 34 deep. $18,000-19,000. 18,500 E

288. Bookcase, circa 1820, Rhineland, ash, pear, three glazed doors, ebonized and gilded pilasters with busts, cornice molding, bronze hardware. 171 cm high, 189 wide, 60 deep. $7,500-9,000. 8,000 E

290

291

292

289. Bookcase, circa 1820, Nuremberg, cherry, pear, two glazed doors, mirror above, gold painting, panels below, flanking ebonized columns set in at the sides, triangular gable. 182 cm high, 125 wide, 40.5 deep. $18,500-20,000. 19,000 E

290. Bookcase, circa 1820, Franconia, cherry, two glazed doors with Gothic pointed-arch bars, flanking ebonized half-columns, also in the center, triangular gable, 238 cm high, 157 wide, 42 deep. $8,000-9,500. 9,000 E

291. Bookcase, circa 1825, Franconia, oak, two doors glazed above with ebonized bars, ebonized columns,, cornice molding. 184 cm high, 121 wide, 531 deep. $3,500-4,000. 4,000 E

292. Bookcase, circa 1840, Bamberg, cherry, two doors glazed above, rectangular panels below, cornice molding with rounded corners. 181 cm high, 125 wide, 42 deep. $6,500-7,000. 7,000 E

289

294

295

296

293

The glass shelves of bookcases were often covered with cloth, usually of a solid color.

293. Bookcase, circa 1820, Fulda, Court Cabinetmaker Arend's shop, cherry, two doors glazed above, panels below, cornice molding with low top, inlaid ebonized shield-shaped escutcheons. 210 cm high, 148 wide, 45.5 deep. $16,500-19,500. 18,000 E

294. Bookcase, circa 1840, Thuringia, cherry, two doors glazed above, panels below, inlaid oval bone lock shields, projecting triangular gable. 187 cm high, 111 wide, 59 deep. $9,500-10,500. 10,000 E

295. Bookcase, circa 1815, Weimar, massive and veneered mahogany, two doors, glazed above with oval and diagonal bars, panels below with raised diamond shapes, cornice molding, original brass hardware. 162 cm high, 92 wide, 32 deep. $11,000-12,500. 12,000 E

296. Bookcase, circa 1820, Thuringia, cherry, two doors glazed above, panels in lower third, two bottom drawers, triangular gable. $15,000-17,000. 16,000 E

297

298

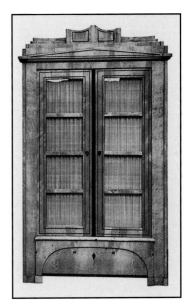

299

The depth of bookcases is much less than that of showcases.

297. Bookcase, circa 1825, Thuringia, walnut, two glazed doors with opposed semicircles, rectangular panels below, cornice molding. $6,500-7,500. 7,000 E

298. Bookcase, circa 1825, Thuringia, birch, two glazed doors, bottom drawer, flanking inset columns with ebonized capitals and bases, stepped top with triangular gable. $5,500-7,000. 6,000 E

299. Bookcase, circa 1835, northern Saxony, partly ebonized, two glazed doors, flanking columns on blocks, false bottom drawer with arch pattern, multiple-stepped top, triangular gable. 178 cm high, 112 wide, 51 deep. $5,000-7,000. 6,000 E

300. Bookcase, circa 1835, Thuringia, cherry, two glazed doors with pointed-arch bars, cutout bottom, cornice molding. 172 cm high, 110 wide, 42 deep. $8,000-10,000. 9,000 E

300

302

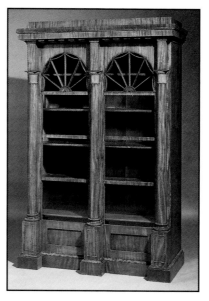

303

304

301

301. Showcase, circa 1825, Berlin, mahogany, glazed on three sides, flanking inset columns with gilded capitals and bases, bottom drawer with two recessed diamond shapes, cornice molding with steps. 177 cm high, 90 wide, 50 deep. $12,500.14,000. 13,000 E

302. Bookcase, circa 1825, northern Germany, mahogany, two glazed doors with arches, rectangular panels in lower quarters, cornice molding with triangular gable. 274 cm high, 100 wide, 33 deep. $5,500-6,500. 6,000 E

303. Bookcase, circa 1825, Lower Saxony, mahogany, two glazed doors with star-shaped decor in upper third, flanking inset columns on base blocks, also in the center, top with toothed frieze. $10,000-14,000. 12,000 E

304. Showcase, circa 1840, Saxony, mahogany, maple, glassed on three sides, bottom drawer, multi-stepped top with triangular gable, maple fillets. $4,500-6,000. 5,000 E

305   306

Corner showcases were popular in Biedermeier times to structure the room additionally and gain space, especially for chinaware and glassware.

305. Corner showcase, circa 1825, Brandenburg, birch, two doors below, twoi glazed doors above, storage spaces flanked by scrolls, cornice molding, inlaid shield-shaped escutcheons. 215 cm high, 110 wide, 80 deep. $6,000-7,500. 7,000 E

306. Corner showcase, circa 1820, Westphalia, ash with ebonized contours, glazed door above, panel below, inlaid shield-shaped escutcheons. 220 cm high, side depth 75 cm. $4,500-5,500. 5,000 E

307. Corner showcase, circa 1820, northern Germany, birch, glazed door above, door with panel below, triangular gable, inlaid shield-shaped escutcheons. 193 cm high, 56 wide, 78 deep. $4,000-5,000. 4,500 E

307

308

309

308. Table, circa 1820, designed by Josef Danhauser, Vienna, cherry, amaranth and maple filet, long rectangular top with rounded corners, double columns at sides, curved four-angled skid feet, knee-high crossbar. 80 cm high, 180 long, 89.5 deep. $12,500-15,000. 14,000 E

309. Table, circa 1820, Vienna, Josef Danhauser circle, cherry, long rectangular top with rounded corners, double columns at sides, curved footbridges linked by round bar, drawer. 74 cm high, 112 wide, 64 deep. $7,000-9,000. 8,000 E

310

310. Table, circa 1820, Vienna, designed by Josef Danhauser, mahogany, maple, oval top, two channeled conical legs tapered in toward the bottom, round bases linked by crosspiece. 79 cm high, 145 wide, 72.5 deep. $24,000-27,500. 25,000 E

311. Table, circa 1835, presumably from Bohemia, owner's mark from Berlin, mahogany, two drawers, long rectangular top with rounded corners, multicurved crossed legs, turned crossbar. 78 cm high, 155 wide, 77 deep. $9,000-10,000. 9,500 E

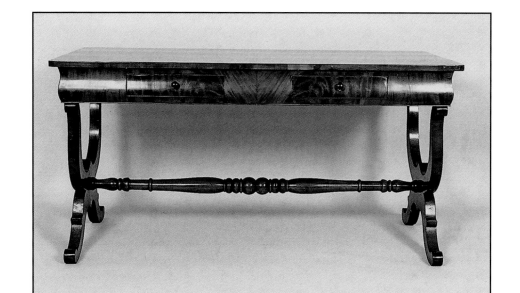

311

312

314

313

315

312. Table, circa 1825, Vienna, walnut, cherry, from the Danhauser Furniture Factory of Vienna, Tea Table no. 11, round top with star-shaped veneer, central marquetry, four Tuscan columns, extended rounded feet, small covered vase on steps. 76,5 cm high, 125 diameter. $7,500-8,000. 8,000 E

313. Table, circa 1820, Vienna, crosscut walnut, round top with star-shaped veneer, channeled middle shaft, round stepped footplate. 71 cm high, 105 cm diameter. 5,000-6,000. 5,500 E

314. Table, circa 1810, Austria, mahogany, three snakes linked as legs and feet, partly gilded, partly green, round top, three-pointed base. 77 cm high, 107 cm diameter. $19,000-20,000. 19,500 E

315. Table, circa 1820, Vienna, walnut, round top, central hexagonal shaft with three curved feet, two braces under the top to prevent warping. 81 cm high, 95 diameter. 5,000-6,000. 5,500 E

316

317

316a

318

316. Pull-out table, circa 1830, Thuringia, walnut, round top with star-shaped veneer, central column with two ebonized profiles, channeled lower part, three-pointed base, two leaves, extendable to five meters. 80 cm high, 125 diameter. $10,000-13,000. 12,000 E

316a. The same table fully extended.

317. Table, made by Master Cabinetmaker Ruckdäschl in Munich, 1834, cherry, round top with star-shaped veneer, central rosette, central column, polygonal lower part, round base with three ebonized feet. 78.5 cm high, 117 diameter. $8,000-9,000. 8,500 E

318. Table, circa 1845, Thuringia, cherry, oval top with star-shaped veneer and fillet stripe, hexagonal central column on multi-curved legs. 79 cm high, 117 wide, 93 deep. $3,900-4,250. 4,000 E

319

321

320

322

319. Table, circa 1835, Baden, walnut, round top, central baluster shaft, scrolled legs. 76 cm high, 119 diameter. $5,000-6,000. 5,500 E

320. Table, circa 1825, Baden, walnut including crosscut, round top with star-shaped veneer, central baluster shaft, three-part foot with scrolls. 72 cm high, 112 diameter. $7,000-8,500. 8,000 E

321. Table, circa 1830, Baden, walnut including crosscut, round top with star-shaped veneer, central baluster shaft, three-part foot with scrolls. $7,000-8,500. 8,000 E

322. Table, circa 1840, Hesse, walnut, round top with star-shaped veneer, grooved rim, central baluster shaft, three curved legs. 76 cm high, 119 diameter. $4,500-5,500. 5,000 E

323

325

324

326

The round table prevents a table hierarchy, for every place is basically of equal value. The family members and guests can gather at the table without worrying about rank and importance.

323. Table, circa 1825, Hesse, walnut, round top, star-shaped veneer, central cornered shaft, three-part foot. $6,000-7,500. 7,000 E

324. Table, circa 1835, Mainz, walnut, round top, round central shaft, three-part foot.
$7,500-8,500. 8,000 E

325. Table, circa 1825, Saxony, mahogany, maple, extendable round top, hexagonal central shaft with three S-shaped legs, three-part foot. 82 cm high, 130 diameter. $8,500-9,500. 9,000 E

326. Table, circa 1820, Thuringia, ash, round top, star-shaped veneer, central three-part foot with gold-leaf dolphins set on it. 78 cm high, 128 diameter. $14,000-16,000. 15,000 E

327

327. Table, circa 1820, Thuringia, walnut, round top, star-shaped veneer, central three-part foot with carved horns of plenty. 78 cm high, 116 diameter. $10,000-12,000. 12,000 E

328. Table, circa 1845, Gotha, inventory stamp of Duke Ernst II of Saxe-Coburg-Gotha, mahogany, maple, round top, central veneer. 72 cm high, 115 diameter. $6,000-7,500. 7,000 E

328

329

329. Table, circa 1815, Vienna, walnut, birch root, diagonally veneered
oval top, birch-root veneer on the edges, drawer, four gilded female
heads, curved legs with curved four-sided middle plate, blackened lion's-
paw feet. 79 cm high, 93 wide, 64 deep. $16,000-19,000. 17,500 E

330

330. Table, circa 1820, southern Germany, cherry, round top, three doubly curved legs, triangular middle plate. 77.5 cm high, 95 diameter. $6,000-7,000. 6,500 E

331. Table, circa 1820, Franconia, cherry, round top, ebonized edge, four curved legs. 78 cm high, 129 diameter. $7,500-8,500. 8,000 E

331

332

332. Table, circa 1825, Hesse, walnut, round top, star-shaped veneer, three doubly curved legs, triangular middle plate with small panel holding printed view of Frankfurt. 78 cm high, 115 diameter. $6,000-7,500. 7,000 E

333. Half-moon table, circa 1820, Baden, walnut, gateleg for the folding panel, drawer, straight four-sided legs. 81 cm high, 119 diameter. $6,000-7,000. 6,500 E

333

334

336

335

337

Light and mobile small tables are elegant in the British style and at the same time practical and useful.

334. Table, circa 1840, Saxony, mahogany, maple, folding panels with felt inlays, baluster shaft with channeling and leaf carving, base with legs ending in carved lions' feet. 79 cm high, 86 long, 43 wide. $2,750-3,500. 3,000 E

335. Table, circa 1820, northern Germany, mahogany, round top, maple frieze, hexagonal central shaft with three double scrolls, three-part base, legs with brass shoes. 76 cm high, 95 diameter. $4,500-5,500. 5,000 E

336. Table, circa 1825, northern Germany, mahogany, long rectangular top with folding side panels, drawer, round central shaft, four-cornered curved-sided footplate with extended scroll feet. 64.5 cm high, 107 wide, 52 deep. $3,000-3,750. 3,000 E

337. Table, circa 1830, northern Germany, mahogany, long rectangular top with folding side panels, two drawers, lyre-shaped pairs of legs with brass bars, curved crossbar, scroll feet with brass casters. $9,000-10,000. 9,500 E

338

339

338a

340

The printing process developed in Britain around 1750, chiefly for the decoration of stoneware, was used there on furniture from about 1790. It was used from 1818 by Georg Hiltl in Munich, with the black print color being transferred from a moistened sticky material by rubbing on a still-damp wooden surface prepared with glue and sand varnish. Then it was saturated with varnish.

338. Table, circa 1820, Vienna, cherry, long rectangular folding top, straight square legs. $3,500-4,500. 4,000 E

338a. Table, circa 1815, Vienna, designed by Josef Danhauser, long rectangular top, straight square cherry legs, partly ebonized. $3,000-4,500. 4,000 E

339. Card table, circa 1820, southern Germany, walnut, long rectangular turning and folding top covered with felt, pointed square legs. 78 cm high, 85 wide, 42.5 deep. $3,000-3,500. 3,000 E

340. Table, circa 1820, Munich, walnut, Hiltl workshop, drawer, square top with rich printing, straight square legs. 76 cm high, 84.5 wide, 56 deep. $10,000-12,000. 11,000 E

341

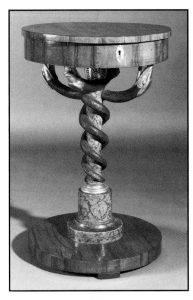

343

342

344

The transition from Empire to Biedermeier was particularly smooth in Viennese furniture.

341. Decorative table, circa 180-5, Vienna, mahogany veneer on maple and fir, marquetry in mahogany and etched pear, carved parts set and gilded, original hardware, four winged Egyptian female figures surround tapered central foot, four-cornered bottom. 76.5 cm high, 58 wide, 44 deep. $30,000-32,500. 31,000 E

342. Decorative table, circa 1810, Vienna, walnut, partly carved and oil-gilded, drawer, four curved legs ending in rams' heads, partly gilded, oval top and bottom plate, original brass hardware. 77 cm high, 63.5 wide, 48 deep. $6,000-8,000. 7,000 E

343. Decorative table, circa 1820, Vienna, walnut, central marbleized shaft, surrounded by four fully three-dimensional snakes, gilded heads, drawer, round top and bottom plate. 82 cm high, 54.5 diameter. $9,000-10,500. 10,000 E

344. Decorative table, circa 1815, Vienna, mahogany, bowl-shaped round top with hexagonal inlaid lid, three curved caryatid legs, set and oil-gilded, hanging bowl in the center, three-part base with concave sides. 74 cm high, 46 diameter. $13,000-15,000. 14,000 E

345

347

346

348

345. Decorative end table, circa 1815, southern Germany, cherry, partly gilded, oval top with ebonized inlay, drawer in rim, ebonized saber legs, lions' heads with ebonized manes, four-sided linking panel. 73.5 cm high, 60,0 wide, 42.5 deep. $6,000-7,000. 6,500 E

346. End table, circa 1825, Brandenburg, birch root, round top, ten-pointed star baseplate, column on cubic base, drawer in rim. 75 cm high, 62 diameter. $3,250-3,750. 3,500 E

347. Console table, circa 1815, Thuringia, walnut including crosscut, semicircular top with ebonized central cutout, three elegantly curved legs, sphinx-heads fire-gilded in the center, three-pointed base, fire-gilded leg bases and lion's-paw feet. 83 cm high, 80 wide, 40 deep. $9,000-12,000. 10,500 E

348. Console table, circa 1825, Munich, made by Jean-Baptiste Metivier for Baron von Lotzbeck, Weyhern Castle, cherry, long rectangular gray marble top, rim drawer, four column legs on semicircular feet, foot braces with central junction and two side arches. 82 cm high, 132 wide, 49 deep. $12,000-13,500. 13,000 E

349

350

351

352

353

354

349. Globe table, circa 1815, Vienna, maple, polished and painted black, cut parts green and gold, opening, lavishly designed interior with ornamental marquetry band and hanging pine cone, three elegantly curved legs with lions' heads and paw feet, three-cornered bottom. $30,000-40,000. 35,000 E

350. Sewing table, circa 1820, Thuringia, cherry, hemispherical body, removable interior, three curved legs with rams' heads, round top, three-cornered lower plate. 77 cm high, 49 diameter. $11,000-14,000. 12,500 E

351. Sewing table, circa 1825, northern Germany, mahogany, birch root, oval plate, interior structure made for sewing equipment, four curved legs, lower crossbars meet in a circle. 74 cm high, 56 wide, 43 deep. $2,750-3,750. 3,000 E

352. Sewing table, circa 1820, Kassel, signed "David Deting, Cassel" on inset spindle clock, round top, three curved legs ending in paw feet, three-cornered lower plate. 80 cm high, 45 diameter. $11,000-14,000. 12,500 E

353. Sewing table, circa 1820, northern Germany, walnut, maple including birdseye, round top, four drawers in drum rim, brass knobs, curved legs with arched rungs to round central segment. 77 cm high, 52.5 cm diameter. $3,500-4,500. 4,000 E

354. Sewing table, circa 1835, northern Germany, mahogany, maple, stripe inlays, concave front of top above drawer, hanging sewing bag, four curved legs above plate, channeled baluster foot below with three scrolls and three-cornered base. 75.5 cm high, 54 wide, 39 deep. $2,250-2,750. 2,500 E

355

357

Decoration, prestige and manifold utility often worked hand in hand. Various sewing and handicrafts had their nooks, rolls and drawers. Often a small sack for yarn and other materials was hung on.

355. Sewing table, signed inside the top "Caroline Hayd of Schwabmünchen" (near Augsburg), dated 1829, walnut, cherry inside, colored maple, long rectangular top, compartments inside, four ebonized column feet, rectangular base. 76 cm high, 50 wide, 39 deep. $6,000-7,500. 7,000 E

356. Lyre sewing table, circa 1825, Rhineland, cherry, long rectangular top with two flaps, lyre-shaped sides with ebonized swan heads linked by container, ebonized lions'-feet. $8,000-9,000. 8,500 E

357. Lyre sewing table, circa 1825, Austria, cherry, maple, two drawers, lyre foot, profiled bottom. 74 cm high, 56 wide, 52 deep. $7,500-8,500. 8,000 E

356

359

360

358. Desk, circa 1815, Vienna, designed by Josef Danhauser, cherry, three drawers and two doors in secretary part, drawers and compartments above, gilded bronze hardware. 97 cm high, 101 wide, 63 deep. $65,000-70,000. 67,500 E

359. Desk, model no. 9, circa 1825, Vienna, designed and made at Danhauser's Furniture Factory, drawing of factory is preserved in papers at Vienna MAK, inv. no. kl 8971/LXXIII 1859, cherry veneer on pine, maple, table with oval writing surface stepped at the sides, rim drawer, four legs with balusters on bridges with saber feet, gable-shaped connector, knee-high shelf, concave-cut book-shelf, two open compartments flanked by two drawers on each side, lock shields in form of hearts with wings and garlands. 97 cm high, 101 wide, 63 deep. $29,000-32,000. 30,500 E

360. Desk, circa 1825, Vienna, probably designed by Josef Danhauser, walnut, secretary top with two drawers between two columns, upper front drawer as folding writing panel, half-sliding lid, knee-high shelf, feet end in scrolls at front. 100 cm high, 103 wide, 68 deep. $17,000-19,000. 18,000 E

358

361

363

362

364

361. Desk, circa 1820, Vienna, cherry, mahogany, stripe inlays, mahogany and maple interior, two doors in secretary part flanked by two columns each, three drawers above, roll-top, sliding writing panel, drawers and pigeonholes inside, crowning gallery in back. 100 cm high, 156 wide, 83 deep. $22,500-24,000. 23,000 E

362. Desk, circa 1825, Vienna, ebonized maple, three drawers in secretary part, borne by two channeled columns on bases, turned crossbar, four small compartments joined by steps on writing surface, crowning gallery. 106 cm high, 126 wide, 77 deep. $10,000-11,000. 10,500 E

363. Desk, circa 1825, Austria, walnut, three drawers in writing part, curved legs and bridges. two drawers in top. $10,000-11,000. 10,500 E

364. Desk, circa 1845, Vienna, walnut including crosscut, drawer in writing part, curved side legs with turned tops, crossbar formed of two scroll bridges, two drawers on writing surface flanked by four small drawers, side rails. $14,000-15,000. 14,500 E

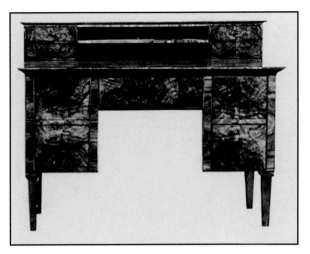

365

366

367

365. Desk, circa 1820, Austria, walnut, two drawers in desk part flanking kneehole, plus middle drawer, boxy top with two compartments flanked by two small drawers each, pointed square legs. 95 cm high, 126 wide, 74 deep. $6,500-8,500. 7,500 E

366. Desk, circa 1845, Bohemia, walnut, rim drawer in desk part, borne by two lyre-shaped side panels, curved crosspiece, boxy top with four small drawers. 92 cm high, 112 wide 62 deep. $7,000-8,000. 7,500 E

367. Desk, signed "Master Ungelehrt" (Unglert), Journeyman Fäustle of Obergünzburg, dated 1841, made either in Saxony or to Saxon model, mahogany, maple, rim drawer in desk part, two baluster legs with carved rosettes and stripe inlays, on channeled bridges, sliding door, drawers inside, large compartment above flanked by two doors. 118 cm high, 125 wide, 72 deep. $15,000-18,000. 16,500 E

368

369

368. Desk, circa 1830, Munich, attributed to Melchior Frank, label of the Bavarian Ministry of War on the underside, cherry, three drawers, turned ebonized legs, inlaid shield-shaped escutcheons. 78 cm high, 121 wide, 62 deep. $12,000-13,500. 13,000 E

369. Desk, circa 1815, probably Munich, cherry, box form with folding top divided in the middle, square pointed legs. 80 cm high, 118 wide, 75 deep. $7,000-8,500. 8,000 E

370. Desk, circa 1820, Upper Bavaria, walnut, three drawers on each side plus middle drawer with central lock, square pointed legs, red leather writing surface worked into the top. 78 cm high, 139 wide, 80 deep. $7,000-8,000. 7,500 E

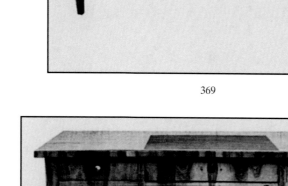

370

371

372

371. Desk, circa 1825, Lower Bavaria, four side drawers and middle drawer over curved kneehole, boxy top with arched central compartment flanked by four small drawers, ebonized edges, curved pointed legs, inlaid shield-shaped escutcheons. 80 cm high, 160 wide, 78 deep. $18,500-19,500. 19,000 E

372. Desk, circa 1815, Upper Bavaria, cherry, four side drawers and middle drawer, raised rim, eight square legs, inlaid ebonized escutcheons. 78 cm high, 160 wide, 60 deep. $12,000-13,000. 12,500 E

373

Desks were often designed, and veneered on all sides, so that they could stand free in a room.

373. Desk, circa 1810, Baden, walnut, four drawers on each side, middle drawer, four projecting half-columns, bases, inlaid leather surface and brass keyhole liners. 75 cm high, 160 wide, 71 deep $12,000-13,000. 12,500 E

374. Desk, circa 1820, Hesse, from Darmstadt Schindelhaus, was rented for life by the Princess of Hesse to the Sternberger family, cherry, three drawers, two doors, gallery with small rail, inlaid ebonized escutcheons, square legs and steps. 84 cm high, 190 wide, 71 deep. $14,000-16,000. 15,000 E

374

375

376

377

375-376. Desk, circa 1815, Neuwied, attributed to Johann Wilhelm Vetter, cherry veneer on fir (body) and oak (drawers), four drawers below, drawer and doors under writing panel, adjustable top section with writing and notating panel, a crank activates three processes, raising and lowering as well as halting of the upper panel, twenty-one oak drawers in all, seven secret compartments, some with springs and hidden locking mechanisms, six drawers in top part, pointed square legs, unusually precise locks and multiple locking, original brass hardware and pull rings. 145 cm high, 133 wide, 66 deep. 32,500-37,500. 35,000 E

377. Secretary, circa 1820, northern Bohemia, walnut including crosscut, birch root, maple, yew, seven drawers below, sliding cover of writing panel, drawers behind it, two shutters above around central lectern, drawers and compartments behind with round arches, secret drawers, ebonized side columns and pilasters with carved and gilded capitals, top drawer with triangular gable, gallery with baluster columns, wall marquetry, carved, gilded and ebonized caryatid pilasters. 204 cm high, 142 wide, 80 deep. $70,000-80,000. 75,000 E

378

380

379

381

378-379. Desk, circa 1805, Neuwied, attributed to Johann Wilhelm Vetter, mahogany veneer on oak and yew, two drawers with two flanking doors, writing panel, drawers behind it, top adjustable via crank, lavish original fire-gilded locks. 84 cm high closed, 128 wide, 63 deep. $32,500-36,000. 34,000 E

380. Secretary, circa 1820, northern Germany, mahogany, two doors below, three drawers behind, crosspiece in kneehole, writing panel, three central drawers above flanked by two doors, inlaid brass escutcheons. $12,000-14,000. 13,000 E

381. Secretary, circa 1820, northern Germany, from Carlshof Castle in Darmstadt, mahogany, two doors below, three drawers behind, secretary structure set back from desk area, writing panel, detailed interior, toothed molding, stepped top with drawer. 148 cm high, 145 wide, 77 deep. $7,000-9,000. 8,000 E

382

383

384

385

386

387

382. Chair, circa 1810, Vienna, ebonized wood, painting on back and frame, bars in back, rail frame design. $7,000-8,000. 7,500 E

383. Six chairs, circa 1815, Vienna, ebonized wood, top rail of the back with gilded decoration, rail frame design. 89 cm high, 48 wide, 40 deep. set $18,000-19,000. 18,500 E

384. Two chairs, circa 1825, Vienna, designed by Josef Danhauser (Chair Model no. 1), stamp and inventory number of Ernst I, Duke of Saxe-Coburg-Gotha, from Rosenau Castle, ebonized cherry, rail frame design. Set $6,000-6,500. 6,500 E

385. Four chairs, circa 1825, Vienna, walnut, maple, rail frame design. Set $14,000-16,000. 15,000 E

386. Six chairs, circa 1830, probably Bad Aussee, so labeled, cherry, back with fan motif, rail frame design. Set $19,000-20,500. 20,000 E

387. Four chairs, circa 1830, Austria, walnut, back with fan motif, rail frame design. Set $12,000-14,000. 13,000 E

388

389

390

391

392

393

388. Four chairs, circa 1835, Austria, cherry, multi-curved scoop backs with turned crossbar, rail frame design. Set $14,000-15,000. 14,500 E

389. Four chairs, circa 1825, Austria, cherry, black lead painting, scoop backs with crossbar, rail frame design. Set $7,000-8,000. 7,500 E

390. Chair, circa 1825, Austria, cherry, scoop back, rail frame design. $1,250-1,750. 1,500 E

391. Two chairs, circa 1820, Vienna, probably designed by Josef Danhauser, mahogany, original finish, rail frame design, part of a set with sofa and armchairs. Set $35,000-40,000. 38,000 E

392. Four chairs, circa 1825, Austria, scoop back with black lead painting, rail frame design. Set $15,000-18,000. 16,500 E

393. Four chairs, circa 1830, Vienna, walnut, ebonized turned crossbar in back, rail frame design. Set $14,000-15,000. 14,500 E

394

395

396

397

394. Chair from seating set, circa 1805, southern Germany, cherry, Gothic back motif, rail frame design. $2,000-2,250. 2,000 E

395. Chair, circa 1805, southern Germany, cherry, pointed oval back motif, rail frame design. 89 cm high. $1,500-1,800. 1,500 E

396. Two chairs, circa 1805, southern Germany, cherry, turned crossbar in upper back, diamond pattern in the middle, bars below, rail frame design. Set $3,000-4,000. 3,500 E

397. Eight chairs, circa 1805, southern Germany, from Hohenaltheim Castle, listed in inveotories since 1807, cherry and pear, massive and veneered on oak. 88 cm high, 46 wide, 42 deep. Set $24,000-26,000. 25,000 E

398

399

400

398. Five chairs, circa 1805, Regensburg, from Prince-Primate's Residence in Regensburg, later Ringler family, walnut, massive and veneered on pine, original belting and upholstery, inventory numbers R 15, R 23, R 24 written in black on the belting, front rails veneered in mirror pattern over central joint, Gothic rail in lower back, back rails of massive walnut, showing that the chairs were made to be seen from the front (elegant placement along a wall), only the hemp belts and the linen covering above remain of the original upholstery, rail frame design. Set $19,000-21,000. 20,000 E

399. Four chairs, circa 1825, Upper Bavaria, cherry, shoulderpiece with ebonized edge, rail frame design. 91 cm high, 42.5 wide, 40 deep. Comparable chairs are seen in Princess Mathilde's salon at trhe Munich Residence (interior by Lorenzo Quaglio) and the billiard room of King Max Joseph at Nymphenburg (interior by Friedrich Ziebland). Set $7,000-8,000. 7,500 E

400. Two chairs, circa 1835, Munich, stamped HME (Duke Max Emanuel), from Biederstein Castle, elm, massive and veneered. Set. $5,500-6,500. 6,000 E

401. Six chairs, circa 1820, probably Munich, cherry, crescent atop vertical trapezoid p[anel in back, black lead painting. 47.5 cm high, 44.6 wide, 42 deep. Set $18,000-19,000. 18,500 E

401

402

403

404

405

402. Two chairs, circa 1810, Würzburg, from the Residence there, various inventory labels, cherry, ebonized half- and quarter-circular bars in back, rail frame design. Set $6,000-7,000. 6,500 E

403. Six chairs, circa 1820, western Lower Franconia, veneered and massive walnut, vertical trapezoid decor in back, rail frame design. 90 cm high, 45 wide, 42 deep. Set $13,000-14,000. 13,500 E

404. Four chairs, circa 1825, western Lower Franconia, ash root, ebonized bars in variant of the Prince of Wales' emblem, rail frame design. Set $8,000-9,000. 8,500 E

405. Four chairs, circa 1830, western Lower Franconia or Hesse, cherry, drapery in black lead painting on back, rail frame design. Set $15,000-17,000. 16,000 E

407

408

409

406. Six chairs, circa 1825, Aschaffenburg, from royal castle there, walnut veneer on walnut, upholstered back, rail frame design. Set $21,000-22,000. 21,500 E

407. Two chairs, circa 1820, Middle Franconia, cherry, crest, vase-shaped decor with black lead painting, rail frame design. Set $4,000-4,500. 4,000 E

408. Four chairs, circa 1820, western Lower Franconia, cherry, walnut, crest partly ebonized, two ebonized scrolls in back, rail frame design. 47 cm high, 44 wide, 45.5 deep. Set $9,000-10,000. 9,500 E

409. Two chairs, circa 1820, Franconia, cherry, walnut, concave central tongue blends into bowed crest board, rail frame design, 86 cm high, 45.5 wide, 48 deep. set $3,500-4,000. 3,500 E

406

410

411

413

412

410. Two chairs, circa 1830, Hesse, walnut, scoop shoulderboard, lyre motif, rail frame design. Set $2,500-3,000. 2,800 E

411. Four chairs, post-1816, Frankfurt, Habsburg state furniture to furnish the chambers of the Austrian embassy to the German Federation at the Thurn and Taxis Palace in Frankfurt on the Main, inventory label "Austria No. 210", massive and veneer walnut on beech, portrayal of a hand mirror with snake carved into the back as an allegory of Prudentia before crossed sword and scepter insignia, rail frame design. 88.5 cm high, 49 wide, 53 deep. Set $25,000-30,000. 28,000 E

412. Two chairs, circa 1820, Frankfurt, probably by Johann Valentin Raab, at Villa Knoll, Stuttgart, cherry, back partly ebonized, Imperial eagle standing on four pillars, rail frame design, 85 cm high, comparable piece at Berchtesgaden Castle. Set $5,000-6,000. 5,500 E

413. Twelve chairs, circa 1815, Frankfurt, signed RAAB (Johann Valentin Raab) on lower frame, princely crown with initials LTL, at Hohengeroldseck Castle, owned by Prince von der Leyen and zu Hohengeroldseck, documented at Waal Castle in 1820, massive and veneer cherry on beech, framed middle field of back with trophy motif, Amazon shield with crossed swords behind, rail frame design, 85 cm high, 46.5 wide, 45 deep. The horizontal frame veneer all around is typical of Frankfurt. Set $40,000-50,000. DM, 45,000 E

414

415

416

414. Four chairs, circa 1815, Frankfurt, mahogany, arch, columns and stylized flower in back, rail frame design. Set $12,500-17,000. 15,000E

415. Two chairs, circa 1820, Frankfurt, cherry, lyre-shaped central tongue with fine fan ornamentation in back, rail frame design. Set $3,500-4,000. 3,500 E

416. Chair, circa 1820, Frankfurt, mahogany, crossed arrows behind central tongue below crest, rail frame design. $1,500-2,000. 2,000 E

417. Six chairs, circa 1825, Hesse, owned by nobility, massive and veneered cherry, ebonized reed-leaf decoration under oval crest with ebonized edge, rail frame design. 91 cm high, 46 wide, 44 deep. Set $18,000-19,000. 18,500 E

417

418

419

420

421

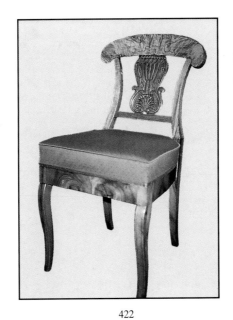

422

Scoop chairs have a wide concave back, bowed and rounded off in scrolls at the sides.

Reed-leaf decoration is a three-part, often ebonized type of decor, its form originating in the feathers of the Prince of Wales as adapted by the British furniture industry. It was already common in Britain in the 18th century.

418. Four chairs, circa 1825, Palatinate, walnut, trapezoid tongue undercrest, rail frame design. 87 cm high. Set $7,000-9,000. 8,000 E

419. Six chairs, circa 1835, Mainz, walnut, pierced central tongue with carving in back, ensemble with two armchairs, sofa and table. Set $42,500-47,500. 45,000 E

420. Chair, circa 1820, Mainz, massive and veneered cherry, gilding, ebonized rectangular inset in crest with two sphinxes, three-part reed-leaf decoration above, rail frame design. 91.5 cm high, 49 wide, 50 deep. $3,250-3,400. 3,300 E

421. Three chairs, circa 1835, Mainz, walnut, lyre-shaped back with curved crest and floral rail-frame design, carvings. 88 cm high. The backs of furniture from the Palatinate often end in scrolls. Set $5,000-6,500. 6,000 E

422. Chair, circa 1835, Mainz, walnut, central tongue with carvings as scoop below curved crest. 86 cm high, 48 wide, 43 deep. $1,600-1,900. 1,750 E

423

424

425

423. Four chairs, circa 1832, Mainz, signed Knussmann, mahogany, slightly curved crest, two crossbars with carved decor, straight turned front legs in British style, rail frame design. 91 cm high, 47 wide, 44 deep. Set $6,000-7,000. 6,500 E

424. Six chairs, circa 1835, Mainz, massive and veneered cherry, lyre-shaped carving on crest, carved middle crossbar, rail frame design. 58 cm high, 44 wide, 42 deep. Set $11,000-12,000. 11,500 E

425. Six chairs, circa 1825, Rhineland, massive cherry, turned bar at top of back, stylized reed-leaf decor radiating from rosette, rail frame design. Set $11,000-12,000. 11,500 E

426. Six chairs, circa 1830, Rhineland, walnut, gondola-shaped backs with rounded top ending in scrolls, fan-shaped central tongue of stylized reed leaves (French influence in western Germany). 88 cm high, 43 deep. Set $12,500-14,000. 13,000 E

426

428

429

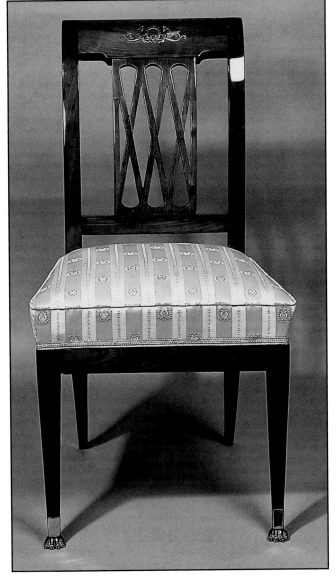

427

427. Six chairs, circa 1815, Baden, mahogany, crossed bars in back, fire-gilded hardware and sabots, rail frame design. Set $17,000-19,000. 18,000 E

428. Chair, circa 1820, Baden, walnut including crosscut, maple, ebonized bar and six rods in back, rail frame design. $1,500-1,800. 1,800 E

429. Six chairs, circa 1820, Karlsruhe, cherry, maple, crossed bars with three small ebonized circles in back, rail frame design. Set $12,000-18,000. 17,500 E

430

431

432

430. Two chairs, circa 1830,
Thuringia, cherry, oval with central
flower developing out of crossbar in
back, rail frame design. Set $3,500-
4,500. 4,000 E

431. Chair, circa 1825, Thuringia.
walnut, corner wedges formed by
arc in back, two crossbars with
semicircle and gilded carving, rail
frame design. 90 cm high. $1,400-
1,700. 1,600 E

432. Two chairs, circa 1825,
Thuringia, mahogany, four-pointed
panel in back with flowers and
central rosette, rail frame design.
Set $3,500-4,000. 4,000 E

433. Four chairs, circa 1820,
Saxony-Anhalt, massive ash, inlaid
lines, ebonized central rosette in
back. Set $7,000-8,000. 7,500 E

433

435

436

In the side frame design, the seat is not resting on the rail frame but is inset into it. This type of design spread from Britain to northern Germany and Scandinavia.

434. Six chairs, circa 1815, Saxony-Anhalt, mahogany on oak, central crossbar in back with metal ornamentation, rail frame design. 86 cm high, 45 wide, 49 deep. Set $12,500-15,000. 14,000 E

435. Chair, circa 1832, inventory label from Altenburg Castle, Duke Ernst, mahogany, carved, doubly curved central crossbar, side frame design (British influence). $2,000-2,500. 2,000 E

436. Three chairs, circa 1825, Saxony-Anhalt, birch, horizontal reed-leaf decoration in back with central rectangle, rail frame design. 97 cm high. Set $4,500-5,500. 5,000 E

434

437

439

440

Saber legs have a shape reminiscent of a saber blade. They were used by British and French designers, based on antique models.

437. Two chairs, circa 1825, northern Germany, mahogany, central tongue of back in form of a double sheaf of grain, channeled round legs, rail frame design. 85 cm high. Set $2,500-4,000. 3,000 E

438. Two chairs, circa 1830, northern Germany, mahogany, curved crest, channeled middle crossbar, turned front legs in British style, side frame design. Set $2,500-3,500. 3,000 E

439. Four chairs, circa 1840, Brandenburg, mahogany, maple, multi-curved crest, central crossbar with circle and flanking acanthus flowers, side frame design. 90 cm high, 41 deep. Set $5,000-6,000. 5,500 E

440. Chair, circa 1828, Stuttgart, Klinkerfuss, from Rosenstein Castle, mahogany, gondola back with shield-shaped piercing, side frame design, saber legs. 88 cm high, 45 wide, 41 deep. $2,500-3,000. 3,000 E

438

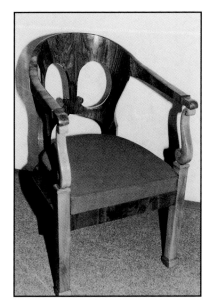

441

442

443

441. Two armchairs, circa 1830, Austria, walnut, back with fan motif. Set $9,000-10,000. 9,500 E

442. Two armchairs, circa 1830, Austria-Hungary, mahogany, curved back and arms with inset scrolls. Set $9,000-10,000. 9,500 E

443. Two armchairs, circa 1815, Vienna, walnut, upholstered headboard, legs made of two intersecting semicircles. 73 cm high, 37.5 wide, 56 deep. Set $11,000-12,000. 11,500 E

444

446

447

Austro-Hungarian seating furniture is often characterized by a light, elegant form and imaginative back designs.

444. Armchair, circa 1825, Vienna, walnut, curved back and arms with inset scrolls. 90 cm high. $3,250-3,750. 3,500 E

445. Two armchairs, circa 1825, Vienna, walnut, arms ending in scrolls. Set $9,000-10,000. 9,500 E

446. Six armchairs, circa 1835, Vienna, cherry, original finish and upholstering. 114 cm high, 84 wide, 93 deep. Set $20,000-22,500. 21,000 E

447. Bergere, circa 1825, Vienna, walnut, curved back and arms with inset scrolls. 92 cm high. $4,000-5,000. 4,500 E

445

448

450

451

449

448. Armchair, circa 1815, southern Germany, cherry, ebonized claw feet, lavishly carved and partly ebonized lion heads, rail frame design. 89.5 cm high, 61 wide, 67 deep. $7,000-7,500. 7,000 E

449. Two elegant armchairs, circa 1805, Regensburg, cherry on soft wood and beech, originally mahoganized, polished, the two front legs form one-footed lion figures with the arms resting on them, probably carved by the Regensburg sculptor Christoph Itelsperger, 1763-1842, original fire-gilded bronze hardware, original belting and [Bourlet], high-class armchairs often have such fringe. 91.3 cm high, 57.5 wide, 60/65.5 deep. Set $90,000-95,000. 92,500 E

450. Two armchairs, circa 1835, Munich, Franz Xaver Fortner, 1798-1877, from Biederstein Castle, elm and rosewood veneer on beech and spruce, set includes four gondola chairs, table, sofa, made for ther King of Bavaria's doctor. Set $45,000-50,000. 47,500 E

451. Armchair, circa 1820, Thuringia, ash, curved arms ending in lion heads. $4,000-4,500. 4,000 E

452

453

455

Sets of chairs and other furniture are rare and are worth considerably more than the values of the individual pieces. Sets are often broken up as a result of divided inheritances or losses from external circumstances.

452. Armchair, circa 1820, Hesse, walnut, arms ending in scrolls, stripe inlays. 86.5 cm high. $2,500-3,000. 3,000 E

453. Armchair, circa 1810, Thuringia, fruitwood, two decorative rods as back-to-back arcs in the back. 92 cm high. $2,500-3,250. 3,000 E

454. Two armchairs, circa 1835, Mainz, walnut, part of group in #419. Set $6,000-7,000. 6,000 E

455. Armchair, circa 1815, Nuremberg, walnut, birch, shoulderboard decorated with dolphins and fan marquetry, paw feet. 6,500-7,500 DM, 3,500 E

454

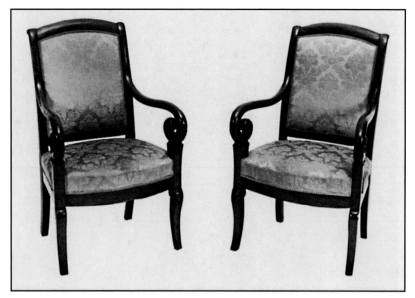

456

457

458

459

460

Bergeres are armchairs with closed arms and full upholstery. They often have extra upholstering provided by a loose cushion in the French style.

456. Two armchairs, circa 1835, Rhineland, mahogany, back with bowed top, scroll arms. set $6,000-7,000. 6,500 E

457. Armchair, circa 1820, Rhineland, walnut, upholstered back. $2,500-3,500. 3,000 E

458. Armchair, circa 1840, Rhineland-Palatinate, cherry, scroll arms, swan-heads on back, built-in adjusting mechanism. $6,000-6,500. 6,000 E

459. Two bergeres, circa 1825, Rhineland, fruitwood, rounded back, arms ending in dolphin heads. 84 cm high. Set $7,500-9,000. 8,000 E

460. Three armchairs, circa 1825, Westphalia, ash, black lead painting, scroll arms, 92 cm high. Set $10,000-13,000. 12,000 E

461

462

463

464

465

466

461. Armchair, circa 1835, Westphalia, birch, scroll arms. $3,500-4,000. 4,000 E

462. Armchair, circa 1830, Berlin, birch, ebonized, back with semicircular cutout and turned top rail, two flanking gold winged lions. $3,500-4,500. 4,000 E

463. Armchair, circa 1825, northwestern Germany, walnut, fan-patterned middle crosspiece. 91 cm high. $2,900-3,500. 3,000 E

464. Armchair, circa 1830, northern Germany, walnut, curved shoulderboard, flat middle crosspiece. $2,500-3,000. 3,000 E

465. Two armchairs, circa 1830, northern Germany, mahogany, flat middle crosspiece, under British influence. Set $5,000-6,000. 5,500 E

466. Two armchairs, circa 1825, Denmark, mahogany, birch, turned legs, channeled arms, decorative bars, under British influence. 85 cm high. $4,500-5,500. 5,000 E

467

468

469

467. Sofa, circa 1810, Vienna, ebonized wood, painting on back, arms ending in partly gilded, partly bronze sphinxes. 100 cm high, 198 wide, 72 deep. $30,000-32,000. 31,000 E

468. Sofa, circa 1815, Vienna, mahogany, carved, partly gilded dolphins on arms, reconstructed original fabric, legs of semicircles crossing each other. 89 cm high, 154 wide, 70 deep. $20,000-22,000. 21,000 E

469. Sofa, circa 1825, Vienna, designed by Josef Danhauser, mahogany, original fabric, see ensemble no. 391. $13,000-15,000. 14,000 E

470

471

472

470. Day bed, circa 1825, Vienna, pencil signature Bullock, dated 1836 on frame, cherry, original etched mahogany, scroll legs. $7,500-8,500. 8,000 E

471. Sofa, circa 1820, Vienna, maple and mahogany veneer on spruce, central foot, all upholstered, paw feet. 100 cm high, 194 wide, 70 deep. $22,500-24,000. 8,000 E

472. Sofa, circa 1825, Vienna, very curved back with fan patterns, linked by turned bar, arc segment below, 104 cm high, 190 wide, 69 deep. $18,000-19,000. 18,500 E

473

474

475

473. Sofa, circa 1815, Vienna, cherry, top of back forms three sides, all upholstered, ebonized inset flanking columns atop high square legs. 98 cm high, 148 wide, 70 deep. $8,000-10,000. 9,000 E

474. Sofa, circa 1825, Vienna, walnut, maple, inset ebonized half-columns on high four-sided legs. $10,000-12,000. 11,000 E

475. Sofa, circa 1825, Vienna, cherry, mahogany, back in scroll form leading to arms, forming two circles below, marquetry on mahogany, all upholstered in cloth. 93,5 cm high, 163 wide, 78 deep. $14,000-15,000. 14,500 E

476

477

476. **Sofa,** circa 1820, Viennan crosscut walnut, straight back with two scroll-shaped wings, flanking ebonized columns with bases and capitals of hammered brass. 98 cm high, 190 wide, 74 deep. $10,000-11,000. 10,500 E

477. **Day bed,** circa 1820, Austria-Hungary, ebonized wood, bars in rails, four-sided pointed feet, 200 cm wide, 80 deep. $13,000-14,000. 13,500 E

478. **Sofa from a set,** 1837, Innsbruck, Johann Nepomuk Geyer, mahogany, maple inpays, carving, scrolls under rounded arms. $11,000-14,000. 12,500 E

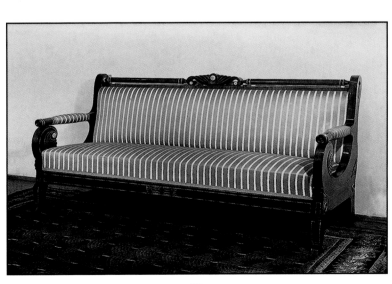

478

479

480

481

479. Sofa, circa 1830, Munich, massive and veneered cherry, from Biederstein Castle, scrolls swinging toward each other on back, , ebonized half-round panels, turned rosettes, black lead painting, stamped "Bairisch Zell" on insides of bars plus inventory number 36b/Hu. Ja (Schnorrstr. 2/4 1).107 cm high, 172 wide, 63 deep. $11,000-13,000. 12,000 E

480. Sofa, circa 1825, Upper Bavaria, cherry, curved back and sides, conical four-sided legs curving outward. 103 cm high, 196 wide, 70 deep. $7,500-8,500. 8,000 E

481. Sofa, circa 1820, Upper Bavaria, walnut including crosscut, curved arms, straight shoulderboard, all upholstered, conical four-sided legs curved outward, 99 cm high, 174 wide, 61 deep. $6,000-7,500. 7,000 E

482

Expensive upholstery fabrics were often protected from sunlight, dust and other wear through the use of a slipcover.

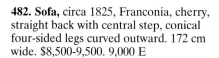

482. Sofa, circa 1825, Franconia, cherry, straight back with central step, conical four-sided legs curved outward. 172 cm wide. $8,500-9,500. 9,000 E

483. Sofa, circa 1830, Franconia, from Biederstein Castle, straight back with central step closed with ebonized rounding, curved sides, conical four-sided feet. 96 cm high, 172 wide, 72 deep. $13,500-15,000. 14,000 E

483

484

485

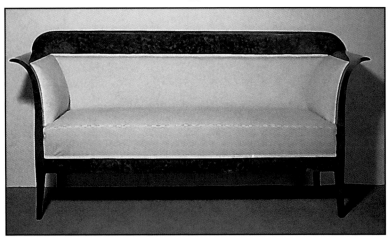

486

484. Sofa, circa 1820, Franconia, cherry, black lead painting, curved sides ending in legs, straight back. 78 cm high, 186 wide. $9,000-10,000. 9,500 E

485. Sofa, circa 1825, Franconia, cherry, bars in sides, straight back, conical four-sided legs. $8,500-9,500. 9,000 E

486/ Sofa, circa 1825, Franconia, cherry, curved sides ending in legs, straight back, conical four-sided legs. $6,500-7,500. 7,000 E

487

488

487. Sofa, circa 1815, Franconia, cherry, straight back, curved arms resting on partly gilded lions, ebonized bars, curved legs. $12,500-13,500. 13,000 E

488. Sofa, signed on a crossbar Ansbach. June 23n 1838, built by Jean Schmidt, decorator, Ansbach, doubly curved sides, slightly curved back, very curved legs. 101 cm high, 200 wide, 71 deep. $9,000-10,000. 9,500 E

489. Sofa, circa 1825, Hesse, walnut, straight back, curved sides with integrated cushions, straight lower panels. $6,000-7,500. 7,000 E

489

490

492

491

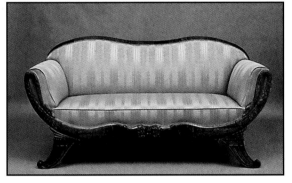

493

Upholstery materials of high quality were very expensive in the Biedermeier era. Often the value of the fabric exceeded that of the furniture. The original fabrics of the time were often of one vivid color, but there were also stripes and other patterns. Cotton and cretonne materials, rep, horsehair, colored leather, oilcloth and, for very expensive furniture, silk were used. Sometimes coverings of canvas and petit-point embroidery were used.

490. Sofa, circa 1830, Thuringia, cherry, curved arms, back and feet. 122 cm high, 224 wide, 171 deep. $6,000-7,000. 6,500 E

491. Sofa, circa 1840, Thuringia, cherry, multicurved back, arms with S-curves, curved feet. $5,500-7,000. 6,000 E

492. Sofa, circa 1840, Palatinate, walnut including crosscut, stepped back, arms with horns of plenty, doubly curved feet. $7,500-8,500. 8,000 E

493. Sofa, Mainz, signed Anton Berger, dated October 12, 1830, walnut, multicurved back, swan's-neck arms. 102 cm high, 209 wide, 17 deep. $8,500-10,500. 9,500 E

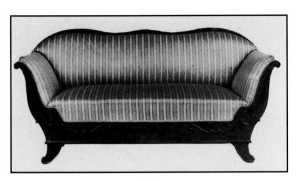

494

496

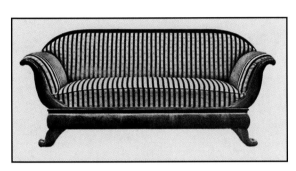

495

497

The so-called Biedermeier fabric with flower patterns was not customary in that era and came into use only after 1895, based on patterns of Louis-Seize clothing and drapery materials. Horsehair upholstery was common. The appearance of the upholstery is important for the total form of the seating furniture.

494. Sofa, circa 1835, Mainz, walnut, multicurved back, curved arms and legs, relief carvings on the frame. $7,500-8,500. 8,000 E

495. Sofa, circa 1825, Lower Franconia/Hesse, walnut, curved back, scrolled arms, padded seat frame, curved legs. 99 cm high, 225 wide, 70 deep. $4,500-5,500. 5,000 E

496. Sofa, circa 1835, Mainz, walnut, part of set in #419, straight back, curved arms, marquetry. $8,000-9,000. 8,500 E

497. Sofa, circa 1830, Palatinate, walnut, curved arms, straight back, curved feet. $6,000-7,500. 7,000 E

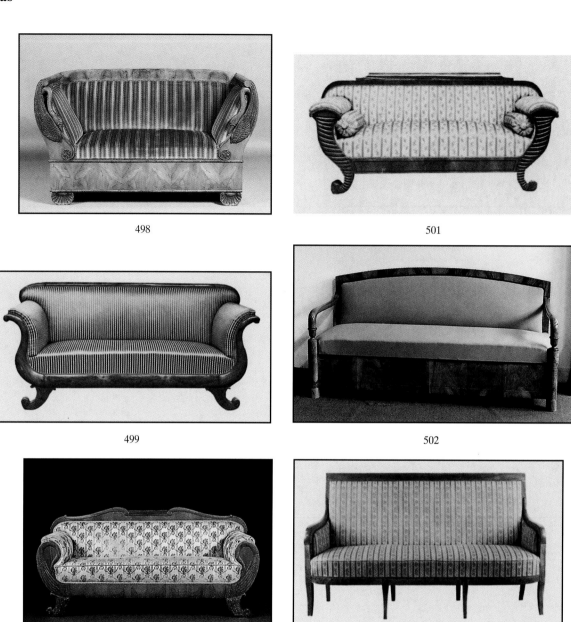

498

501

499

502

500

503

498. Sofa, circa 1825, Rhineland, walnut, swan's-neck arms, richly carved feet, slightly curved back, straight lower frame, sea-shell feet. $8,000-10,000. 9,000 E

499. Sofa, circa 1835, Rhineland, cherry, lyre-shaped frame on feet shaped like horns of plenty. 92 ch high, 145 wide, 62 deep. $6,000-7,000. 6,500 E

500. Sofa, circa 1835, Rhineland, ash, multicurved back, arms with swan's-neck decor. 97 cm high, 207 wide, 60 deep. $6,000-7,000. 6,500 E

501. Sofa, circa 1835, Westphalia, cherry, arms flowing into legs as horns of plenty. 97 cm high, 210 wide. $5,000-6,000. 5,500 E

502. Sofa, circa 1825, Rhineland, walnut, curved arms becoming columnar legs. $6,000-7,000. 6,500 E

503. Sofa, circa 1825, Rhineland, walnut, arms with leaf reliefs, eight curved four-sided pointed feet. 97 cm high, 161 wide, 69 deep. $7,000-8,000. 7,500 E

504

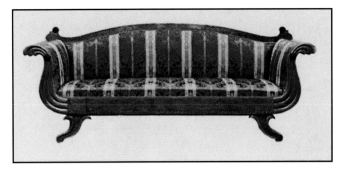

507

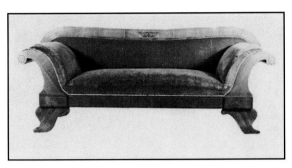

505

508

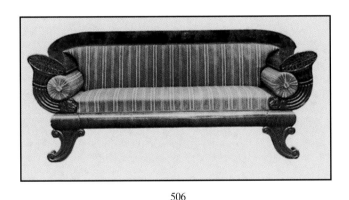

506

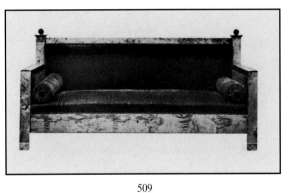

509

Curved backs and arms, carvings and relief ornamentation suited the taste for decoration in the phase after 1835.

504. Sofa, circa 1835, Palatinate, mahogany, arms shaped like horns of plenty with wave and leaf decor, rounded back. 95 cm high, 239 wide, 71 deep. $5,000-6,000. 5,500 E

505. Sofa, circa 1835, Schleswig-Holstein, cherry, decorative field and rosettes on the back and arms. 94 cm high, 245 wide, 70 deep. $5,000-6,000. 5,500 E

506. Sofa, circa 1835, northern Germany, mahogany, arms with horns of plenty ending in lions' heads, fitted-in bolsters, curved back and feet. 98 cm high, 218 wide. $5,500-6,500. 6,000 E

507. Sofa, circa 1845, Denmark, birch, waved arms and feet, curved back. $4,000-5,000. 4,500 E

508. Sofa, circa 1830, Brunswick, mahogany, maple, scroll arms as stylized horns of plenty, fitted-in bolsters, mirror-image mahogany veneer, fine maple inlays, block feet. 97.5 cm high, 213 wide, 70 deep. $10,000-12,000. 11,000 E

509. Sofa, circa 1825, Sweden, birch, straight frame with raised straight back, crowned with two ebonized balls, square feet. 91 cm high, 201 wide, 64 deep. $5,500-6,500. 6,000 E

510

513

511

514

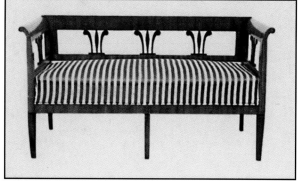

512

515

Benches, unlike sofas, usually have an upholstered seat and open arm and back structure. They offer the possibility of various charming decors, but do not have the sitting comfort of sofas.

510. Bench, circa 1805, southern Germany, ebonized pear, Gothic-style arches in back, stamped brass hardware, curved pointed conical legs, see no. 441. 82 cm high, 168 wide. $4,500-5,500. 5,000 E

511. Bench, circa 1830, southern Germany, ebonized reed-leaf fans set into back, curved arms becoming conical pointed feet. 92 cm high, 178 wide, 55 deep. $3,000-3,500. 3,000 E

512. Bench, circa 1825, southern Germany, cherry, ebonized reed-leaf patterns in back, conical pointed legs. 82 cm high, 158 wide, 60 deep. $2,500-3,000. 2,500 E

513. Bench, circa 1825, southern Germany, cherry, reed-leaf patterns in back, conical pointed legs. 82 cm high, 205 wide, 62 deep. $2,500-3,000. 2,500 E

517

518

519

514. Bench, circa 1820, Franconia, cherry, reed-leaf patterns in back, central flat gable, conical pointed legs. 83 cm high, 148 wide, 61 deep. $3,750-4,250. 4,000 E

515. Bench, circa 1835, Franconia/Thuringia, pear, ebonized lyres in frame, central gabled crown on straight back, curved pointed legs. 103 cm high, 182 wide, 55 deep. $3,000-3,500. 3,000 E

516. Wing chair, circa 1820, Vienna, walnut, wings running to upper angle, flanking half-columns on rectangular bases. $11,000-11,500. 11,000 E

517. Wing chair, circa 1825, Vienna, walnut, wings with S-curve, round legs with step. 118 cm high, 71 wide, 78 deep. $10,000-11,500. 11,000 E

518. Wing chair, circa 1840, southern Germany, cherry, upholstered arms ending in scrolls, conical four-sided legs. $3,500-4,500. 4,000 E

519. Wing chair, circa 1840, Württemberg, oak, back adjustable by leather belts, conical four-sided feet. 129 cm high. $2,500-3,000. 3,000 E

516

520

521

520. Two collection showcases, circa 1810, Munich, veneered and massive cherry, owned by Prince of Thurn und Taxis, St. Emmeran Castle, with inventory number, twelve drawers below, top with gilded dolphins, ebonized columns, gilded lion-paw feet. 225 cm high, 246 wide, 45 deep. Set $80,000-90,000. 85,000 E

521. Etagère, circa 1815, Vienna, mahogany, three inset shelves, carved, partly gilded, partly blackened rams' heads and hooves, bottom plate, stepped top. $15,000-17,000. 16,000 E

522

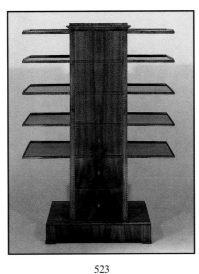

523

524

525

526

527

522. Corner etagère, circa 1820, Vienna, ash, three ebonized round columns at the corners, ending in balls at the top, four inset shelves, eight ebonized arrow-shaped bars. 146 cm high, 47 side length. $10,000-12,000. 11,000 E

523. Etagère, circa 1820, Vienna, in Josef danhauser's style, walnut, six drawers and ten shelves, rectangular base. $17,000-18,500. 18,000 E

524. Etagère, circa 1836, Mainz, Anton Bembe/, [French accent] mahogany, two inset shelves linked by two turned columns with carving and two eagles that carry the top, channeled side pilasters, bottom drawer, row of pearls below it. 168 cm high, 85 wide. $14,000-16,000. 15,000 E

525. Etagère, circa 1835, Mainz, Anton Bembe/, walnut, channeling on back, inset columns with channeled bases, two inset shelves, bottom drawer, channeled feet, scroll top, 175 cm high, 90 wide, 60 deep. $14,000-15,000. 14,500 E

526. Etagère, circa 1835, southwestern Germany, massive and veneered walnut, five shelves rounded at the sides, knobs and rails on top, 134 cm high, 73 wide, 36 deep. $4,000-4,500. 4,000 E

527. Etagère, circa 1825, Vienna, designed by Josef Danhauser, walnut, three shelves between three bowed staves which end in scrolls at top, tapered-in six-cornered foot. 143 cm high, 52 diameter. $16,000-17,000. 16,500 E

528

529

530

531

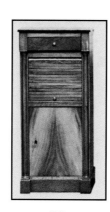

532

533

534

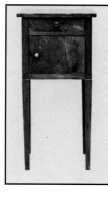

535

536

528. Two drum cupboards, circa 1825, southwestern Germany, cherry, doors, drawer, inset marble tops. Set $5,000. 5,000 E

529. Drum cupboards, circa 1820, Austria, rosewood, door, drawer, marble top, original fire-gilded hardware. $11,500-12,500. 12,000 E

530. Drum cupboard, circa 1825, southern Germany, walnut, door, drawer, sliding blind. set $7,000-8,000. 7,500 E

531. Two nightstands, circa 1820, southern Germany, cherry, door, sliding blind. Set $7,000-8,000. 7,500 E

532. Nightstand, circa 1825, southwestern Germany, walnut, door, shelf with blind, drawer. 79 cm high, 35 wide, 30 deep. $2,000-2,300. 2,000 E

533. Nightstand, circa 1835, southern Germany, cherry, door, drawer, ebonized pilasters. 79 cm high, 35 wide, 32 deep. $1,500-2,000. 2,000 E

534. Nightstand, circa 1820, Rhineland, walnut, door, drawer, flanking inset columns with gilded bases and capitals, protruding top drawer. 86 cm high, 46 wide, 37 deep. $2,000-2,250. 2,000 E

535. Nightstand, circa 1825, southern Germany, walnut, door, drawer. 82 cm high, 42 wide, 36 deep. $1,400-1,750. 1,500 E

536. Nightstand, circa 1820, northern Germany, mahogany, space with blind, false drawer above, top with trembleuse edge. 71 cm high, 35 wide, 34 deep. $1,400-1,750. 1,500 E

537

539

538

540

537. Music stand-table, on an extendable four-sided column with candelabra, labeled: Renotte invenit Expo Bxs 1830, displayed in Brussels in 1830, birch, birch root, central column with carvings and marquetry, swinging bottom compartments, S-shaped legs, when the round top is removed, the table becomes a music stand for a quintet. $15,000-17,500. 16,000 E

538. Music stand, circa 1820, Austria-Hungary, mahogany, lemonwood, fine marquetry, curved conical pointed feet, fine marquetry on the lyre of the music rack. $8,000-9,000. 8,500 E

539. Table piano, circa 1840, southern Germany, cherry, angled baluster legs. $4,500-6,000. 5,000 E

540. Table piano, circa 1830, Heilbronn, signed A. Kulmbach (Friedrich August Kulmbach, 1803-1856), walnut, columnar legs. $5,500-6,500. 6,000 E

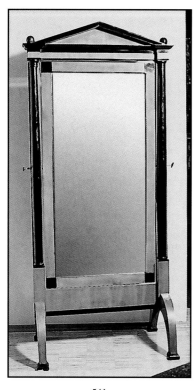

541

542

A psyche is a free-standing frame with a large suspended, swingable mirror. This type of mirror was very popular in the 19th century and very useful to ladies who often had complex wardrobes.

Pillar mirrors are relatively tall and slim mirrors which were hung over bureaus and consoles between two windows. As in the 18th century they served to reflect and intensify the sun- and candlelight in addition to their decorative and practical purposes.

541. Psyche, circa 1825, Franconia, cherry, triangular gable, ebonized edges and knobs, frame with ebonized half-columns, curved legs. 182,5 cm high, 85.5 wide, 53 deep. $7,500-8,500. 8,000 E

542. Psyche, circa 1835, Franconia, cherry, triangular gable, ebonized edges, gilded knobs, ebonized full columns with gilded bases and capitals, doubly curved legs linked with ebonized bar. $5,500-6,000. 6,000 E

543. Psyche, circa 1820, Austria, walnut, gilded oval-line frame, curved legs, conical round columns at the sides, with knobbed crowns of palmette vases, 190 cm high, 107 wide. $5,000-6,000. 5,500 E

544. Psyche, circa 1825, Brandenburg, birch, flanking ebonized half-columns, triangular gable, footplate curved in front, profiling above it. 192 cm high. $3,500-4,500. 4,000 E

543

544

545. Standing mirror, circa 1825, Thuringia, cherry, ebonized field with bronze fitting over the mirror, flanking side channeling, stepped base. $4,000-5,000. 4,500 E

546. Toilet mirror, circa 1820, Brandenburg, cherry, one-drawer box base, curved holder with hanging adjustable oval mirror. 76 cm high. $1,750-2,000. 2,000 E

547. Standing mirror, with console table, circa 1835, Berlin, mahogany, maple, one-drawer frame with white marble plate, scroll legs in front, mirror with flanking half-columns, marquetry tendrils in curved gable top. 100 cm high, 86 wide, 43 deep. $6,000-7,000. 6,500 E

548. Two standing mirrors, with hanging consoles as pillar mirror, circa 1825, Scandinavia, mahogany, maple, rounded one-drawer frame box, flower-vase marquetry below, mirror frame with floral and figured marquetry, antique-style oval in [eglomisee] technique on top, stepped top. 262 cm high, 70.5 wide, 38 deep. Set $12,500-24,000. 13,000 E

546

545

548

547

549

550

551

552

Mirrors were still luxury articles in the Biedermeier era, and were accordingly expensive. With technical advances, larger mirror glass panels could be made, so that the originally technically caused two-part style often disappeared later. Quicksilver was used to make mirrors.

549. Mirror, circa 1820, Rhineland, cherry, ebonized, flanking ebonized half-columns with gilded bases and capitals, carved and gilded hunting scene above, very overhanging cornice molding with gilded frieze of ovals, ebonized footboard with central palmette. $9,000-9,500. 9,000 E

550. Mirror, circa 1825, Rhineland, ebonized and gilded, flanking ebonized half-columns with gilded bases and capitals, ebonized footboard with palmettes, top with Orpheus and his lyre, and a swan at his feet, very overhanging cornice molding with gilded frieze of ovals. 124.5 cm high, 75 wide. $7,500-8,500. 8,000 E

551. Mirror, circa 1820, Rhineland, cherry, footboard with central palmette swings out into the pedestals of the columns, flanking ebonized columns with gilded bases and acanthus capitals, headboard with ebonized field for scene of Diana petting a dog, footboard with central palmette swings out into the pedestals of the columns. 164 cm high, 95 wide. $7,000-7,500. 7,000 E

552. Mirror, circa 1835, Thuringia, mahogany, concave panel, carvings in corners and top, profiled cornice molding. 135 cm, 86 wide. $2,300-2,900. 2,500 E

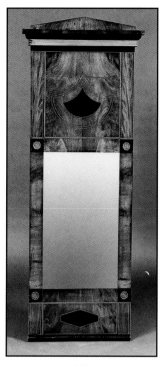

553

554

553. Mirror, circa 1825, Brandenburg, mahogany, maple, stripe inlays, ebonized geometrical fields and panel, bronze rosettes on ebonized corners, triangular gable, 149 cm high, 57 wide. $2,750-3,250. 3,000 E

554. Two mirrors, circa 1820, Franconia, cherry, glassed oval medallion with allegorical figures in gilded relief carving in the upper panel. 133 cm high, 58 wide. Set $5,000-6,000. 5,500 E

555. Mirror, circa 1815, northwestern Germany, mahogany, flanking half-columns with gilded bronze bases and capitals, gilded wooden bar around the attic, architrave with arch, straight top. 193 cm high, 77.5 wide. $2,500-3,250. 3,000 E

556. Mirror, circa 1840, northern Germany, mahogany, divided mirror with flanking scrolls above, gabled top with gilded cyma curve. 95 cm high, 42 wide. $1,500-1,900. 1,500 E

555

556

Glossary

Acanthus: Leaf-shaped decoration on furniture ("acanthus crown") and buildings ("acanthus capital"), named after a plant native to the Mediterranean area and popular because of its beautiful leaves.

Appliqué: Added decorative piece or ornament

Arcade: Arch or row of arches, resting on columns or pillars. The "blind arcade" divides a wall or furniture surface without opening it.

Architrave: Element taken from antique architecture (moulding) that links two columns horizontally.

Archivolte: Element taken from architecture in the form of the top of a round arch.

Atlas: Powerful male figure as beam carrier, counterpart of feminine caryatid.

Baluster: Rounded, very bulging and stocky column, drawn in at the bottom.

Balustrade: A field supported by balusters.

Base: The foot of a column.

Bastion filling: Field filling.

Beech (red beech): Very hard wood used particularly for chair frames and cupboard feet as well as simple furniture.

Bentwood: Wood bent under steam pressure, usually beech. The process was much improved by Michael Thonet around 1840.

Bergère: Form of chair originating in the 18th century, with full upholstery and closed arms, usually with loose seat cushions.

Bevel: Angled surface between two adjoining edges or surfaces. In furniture building, the angling of the edge of a (framed) surface or inset glass.

Blind: Architectonic motif (blind arches, arcades, etc.) set on a body for decoration or sectioning.

Blind wood: Carrier wood, onto which the veneer is glued.

Blocking: design meant to prevent cracking in veneer by keeping movement of the frame to a minimum by opposing the grain direction.

Body: The body of storage furniture, but also the ordinary, not visible blind wood of veneered furniture.

Burnt shadowing: Shadowing effect, especially on maple wood, achieved with hot sand.

Capital: Upper closing of columns, pillars or pilasters.

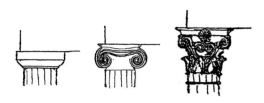

Cartonnier: Rack for writing implements, which can be set on a desk.

Caryatid: Feminine statue as beam carrier in place of a column, counterpart to masculine Atlas.

Chamfer: Reducing the mass of wood by beveling the edges.

Channeling: surface divided by vertical grooves, usually seen in columns and pillar shafts.

Cheek: Vertical, not always closed brace than can take on the function of table legs. The connection be-

tween cheeks can be made by a bridge or rail.

Cherry: Brownish to red-brown hardwood, sometimes with nice graining, used particularly for veneer in the Biedermeier era.

Chiffonier: Pillar bureau, narrow and high, with numerous drawers one over another, usually placed before pillars between windows.

Classicism: Artistic styles based on classical antiquity. Classic style encompassed the period from about 1770 to 1850. The phase before 1800, in which elements of Louis XVI style lived on, is called "Directory" in France after the Directory of the Revolution. The two following decades were generally called Empire on the Continent after the Napoleonic Empire. Roman, Greek and Egyptian motifs appear as art forms. Despite Napoleon's efforts to revitalize various areas of commercial art, artistic handiwork suffered a decline during the French Revolution and the Wars of Liberation. The strongest genre proved to be that of furniture, where the Biedermeier style blossomed.

Column: Round vertical support, consisting of base, shaft and capital.

Column formation: Division of a column into base, shaft and capital.

Console table: Wall table fitted to the space.

Cornice: Upper conclusion of a cupboard, consisting mainly of molding.

Crosscut: Wood cut at a right angle to the direction of the grain.

Crown: Element finishing the vertical extent of a piece of furniture (such as "acanthus crown").

Cushion filling: Better-class "pillow-shaped" filling.

Cylinder bureau (roll bureau): Writing furniture with jalousie or sliding panel in half- or quarter-cylindrical form, developed around 1760. Much rarer in Biedermeier than the writing cabinet (secretary). When opened, the jalousie rolls in between the back wall and sliding box. In a fixed cylinder, the writing surface moves forward when the cylinder is pushed backward.

Cyma (*cymation*, Greek, wave): Decorative molding of stylized leaf shapes.

Diamond stripe: Ornamental stripe with a row of diamond (rhombus) shapes.

Dolphin: Motif used since antique times, often as a support instead of scrolls.

Doubling: gluing boards on each other with grain running in opposed directions, meant to prevent the shrinking and cracking of the wood.

Dovetail joint: Carpenter's technique of making a corner joint, in which alternating tongues grasp each other.

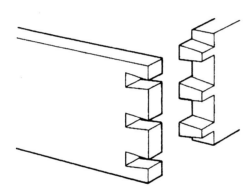

Drum bureau: Bureau or nightstand in the form of a large drum, similar to the column bureau.

Ebonist: Woodworker who uses ebony. Since the 17th Century this has meant an artistic cabinetmaker who chiefly produced veneered furniture.

Ebonizing: Blackening of wood by etching or polishing, done to imitate expensive ebony wood.

Ebony: Collective name for various very dark, heavy and hard exotic woods, often used for fancy furniture because they polish well.

Empire Style: Classic artistic style between 1800 and 1820, established by architects P.F.L. Fontaine (1762-1853) and C. Percier (1764-1838) with their pattern book "Recueil de la décoration interieur". An early phase called "Directoire", named after

the Directory of the French Revolution, was in style from 1790 to 1800. While the influence of Napoleon's Empire resulted in its name on the Continent, in Britain this period was called "Regency", since at that time (1811-1820) George IV served as regent for his sick father George III. While the silhouettes of the most imposing furniture are strict, clear, simple and usually straight-lined, Egyptian, Greek and Roman motifs (sphinxes, griffins, winged steers, lions and horses, urns, wreaths, garlands) were used for decoration. Ornaments like the meander stripe or the oval stripe were also used as ornaments on the fine-grained, usually mahogany-veneered surfaces of furniture.

Etagère: Open set of free standing shelves, or shelves open on three sides and set on other furniture.

Evergreen: Soft, long-fibered woods such as spruce, fir and pine, used primarily in southern Germany and the Alpine lands for early and peasant-type painted furniture. Otherwise they were used mostly as blind wood and thus called "ignoble wood".

Fan: a popular decorative motif used as a rosette or part of one, taken from Renaissance architecture.

Festoon: Decorative motif in the form of a garland or hanging made of flowers, leaves, fruits, often with crosswise bands wound around each other, usually with bands at both ends.

Fiale: Slender, pointed tower, frequent decorative motif of Gothic style.

Field filling: Profiled, elegant filling, resembling stylized fortification designs seen from a bird's-eye view, also called bastion or fortress filling.

Fillet: Diagonal light and dark strips of veneering, usually used as a frieze.

Filling: Thin boards fitted into a groove in a frame so that they can "work" without tearing (as in field filling and pillow filling).

Fir: Type of evergreen tree.

Fittings: Constructive or decorative metal ornaments or hardware on furniture.

Fluting: concave indentation, "hollow throat", especially in moldings, profiles and frames.

Folding star: In furniture, a star-shaped inlay that looks three-dimensional by light-dark contrast.

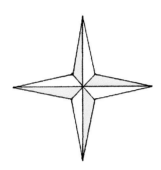

Fortress filling: see field filling.

Frame construction: Design used in central Europe since the Middle Ages, in which a frame of wood is finished with fillings. The weak filling boards have enough play space in the grooves of the strong framework so the wood of the fill-ins can "work" (flex) without cracking.

Frieze: Thin stripes, often used as the edge or frame of a surface, with ornamental or figured decoration.

Furniture: The numerous furnishing articles that have been developed for living and storing. In contrast to the manifold types of moveable furniture, there are few that have been built permanently into a room.

Gable: Roof-like upper closing of furniture, often triangular in Biedermeier style.

Gable field: Facade surface of a gable, often ornamental or with reliefs.

Garland: see festoon.

Gondola chair: Type of armchair with half-round back.

Grain: The pattern and coloring formed by the varying growth of wood fibers. Evergreen woods, for example, are very nicely grained, as are walnut, birch and ash. The veneers taken from the lowermost trunk and roots show especially lively graining. Graining can be intensified by polishing.

Grain veneer: Veneer cut across the trunk, with especially beautiful cloudy forms.

Groove: a longish deepening in which the wedge or tongue piece is placed for attachment. Tongues and grooves were required for frame designs in furniture art.

Gueridon: Decorative high, usually round small table.

Half-column or three-quarter column: Column projecting only halfway (or three quarters of the way) out of the surface (see also column, lisene, pilaster).

Heartwood: Interior of a tree trunk, opposed to the surrounding sapwood.

Hiltl, Johann Georg, first exhibited in his business premises (1818-19) furniture decorated with the graphic printing process brought from Great Britain.

Historicism: Style popular after 1850, followed from 1870 on by Neo-Renaissance, known popularly in Germany as "Old German style". Many articles from this era are still available.

Horn of plenty: Usually curved horn filled with flowers, fruits and the like, symbolizing richness and overabundance.

Hymnal box or bible box: Small cabinet to hold prayer and hymn books, sometimes combined with a prayer stool (Prie-dieu).

Intarsia: Inlaid work of variously colored woods or other materials in massive wood, as opposed to marquetry.

Interior design: Arrangement of numerous drawers, pigeonholes, etc, inside the outer door of a writing or other cabinet.

Joints: Carpentry has developed various means of joining separate pieces of wood during the course of its history, such as nails, gluing and pegging. In the last, equally large holes are bored in the pieces to be joined at places where they intersect, and round dowels are then driven into the holes. Another joining technique is groining, in which the pieces to be joined are cut, one positive, the other negative, so that they can be pushed precisely into each other. In dovetail joints, called dovetail because of their shape, the two pieces are joined by cutting spaces into which the fitted tongues of the other piece will fit, filling them. Boards are joined by tongues and grooves. Further joining techniques include overlapping, slits and tongues, tenons, and wedges.

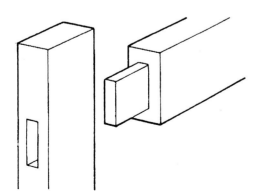

Lisene: Flat vertical projection, usually narrow, of the wall, without base or capital, to divide a surface.

Louis XVI Style: Named for the reign of French king Louis XVI (1774-1792), it began as an artistic style circa 1760. National names such as "queue style" in Germany never became popular. Unlike the previous Rococo, the form of furniture became strict and based on classical influences, as shown also in antique ornaments such as gold cord, wave and meander stripes, and festoons and symbolic ornaments. The composition, especially the marquetry, was refined further, and many renowned ebonists, such as David Roentgen, tried to outdo each other in clever multipurpose furniture. Unlike the lavish furniture of the time, bourgeois Louis XVI furniture often has a simple elegance.

Lyre: Popular motif of Louis XVI and Biedermeier furniture styles, used in chair backs, sewing tables, etc. There were also lyre-shaped secretaries.

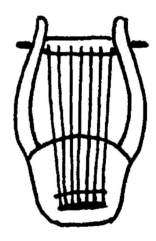

Mahogany: Exotic wood, imported since the late 17th century and used mainly for veneering, since it scarcely splits and can be polished well. First used in France, Britain, Holland and northern Germany, this veneer wood was accepted in the rest of Europe in the reign of Louis XVI and was especially popular in the Empire era.

Marquetry: Variously colored woods or other materials were combined on the blind wood to form ornaments, as opposed to intarsia.

Mascaron: Decorative masks as three-dimensional ornamental elements.

Meander: Ornamental stripe of right-angled lines, from antique sources.

Molding: In furniture, a projecting, usually profiled horizontal element that sections a piece of furniture horizontally, or serves as an upper or lower closing in simple or stepped, profiled form.

Mussel: A seashell motif often used in the Renaissance, Baroque and Rococo styles.

Noble wood: Hardwoods, exotic woods used for veneer, marquetry or intarsia because of their beauty and value.

Oak: Widespread European type of wood, pale brown to brownish-yellow, with clearly marked pores which form lines looking as if made with a needle. One of the hardest woods, it is used massively, left natural, etched, waxed, or used as blind wood and veneered, but seldom used as veneer.

Oval stripe: Antique decorative edge of alternating egg-shaped and pillar-like forms, often bordered above and below by a pearl stripe.

Ox-head chair: Biedermeier chair with a narrower back than the scoop chair, without a tongue.

Palmette: Plant-like ornament with symmetrical fan-shaped leaf arrangements.

Panel: Smooth wooden filling in frame designs.

Paneling: Wooden panels used to cover walls and ceilings.

Paper: Drawers were often lined with a covering of wallpaper.

Pearl stripe: Decorative motif consisting of a row of small pearl-like balls, often used as the upper and lower borders of an oval stripe.

Pilaster: Wall pillar, divided like a column into foot (base), shaft and capital, unlike the lisene.

Pillar: Angular support, as opposed to the always round column, also round supports without bases and capitals.

Pine: Type of evergreen wood.

Polish: Wetting and then treating the veneered surface. Since Biedermeier times the relatively resistant shellac finish has been used.

Polychrome: Colorful, of various colors.

Portico: Projecting front structure supported by columns.

Posament art: Preparation and decorative use of tassels and fringes.

Post: Vertical round or angled wood with a supporting function.

Prie-Dieu: Prayer stool.

Profile: In furniture art this includes moldings, crossbars, etc. of varying form. Smooth boards are profiled with a profiling plane.

Profiling plane: Carpentry tool with which, by using various blades and tool shapes, profiles are planed into wooden pieces.

Projection: Protruding of one element from the surface.

Psyche: An adjustable standing mirror in a frame, widespread in Empire and Biedermeier styles.

Pyramid veneer: It is formed when the cut is guided by the branching of a tree trunk.

Queue style: Style between 1770 and 1795 (Louis XVI style).

Relief (Latin *relevare*, raised): figured or ornamental carvings above the surface level.

Restoration: Art of the Restoration era, 1815-1848.

Rosewood: Hard exotic wood, easily workable, dark brown to violet with deep black veins when cut longitudinally, used in many ways.

Sapwood: Outer part of a tree trunk's wood, usually of different structure than the older heartwood.

Scale veneer: Since the mid-19th century, veneering was no longer sawed but scaled from a turning trunk.

Scoop chair: Typical Biedermeier chair with scoop-shaped back, wide at the top, ending in stylized scroll arms, with a projecting central tongue.

Scroll (volute): Spiral rolled element often used in furniture design, sometimes joining horizontal and vertical members.

Secretary: The popular secretaries of the Louis XVI era, Empire and Biedermeier types go back to the writing cabinets already used in Italy in the 17th century. In the center is a straight writing panel opening to the front, behind it usually a lavish interior with drawers and compartments. The upper part concludes with a small drawer, while the lower part can be a closet with doors or a bureau with drawers.

Settee: Seating furniture for several people, with back and arms.

Shaft: The long middle element of a column, ending in the base and capital.

Showcase: Display case glassed in front and on the sides, with several shelves and often a mirrored rear wall.

Signature: Signed or stamped furniture is of special interest in art history. Pencil signatures were used most often in Biedermeier furniture.

Sofa: Seating furniture appearing at the end of the 17th century, with back and arms, usually holding two or three people.

Spruce: Long-fibered evergreen soft wood, used as blind wood for interior parts and drawers.

Stave work: Slim vertical members, used to divide windows in Gothic style, uniting to form > tracery in an arched field. Often used in the windows of Biedermeier bookcases and showcases.

Strike plate (contact bar): The bar covering the vertical space between two doors, it strikes the body or the other door when the doors are closed.

Stripe inlay: straight-line intarsia or marquetry in which thin strips of light/dark contrast, usually maple or satinwood, were inlaid in mahogany.

Style furniture: Furniture made in a later era with the stylistic features of an earlier era (historicism).

Tabouret: Low upholstered four-legged stool, customary since about 1700.

Tongue: Design element used to unite edges of wood by fitting into a groove. Also a central piece of wood in the frame of a chair back or top rail, often ornamentally formed.

Toothing: Antique decorative crossbar pattern popular in furniture design, made up of a row of small cubic blocks separated by narrow spaces (frieze).

Top rail: Horizontal connector between posts. Usually a narrow hanging bar on furniture, such as under tabletops, at the bottom of bureaus and cupboards, or as a frame member under the seat areas of chairs and sofas.

Tracery: The "measured" decor of Gothic art formed with a compass, an abstract geometrical ornamentation without objective meaning.

Transfer: Process of transferring a copperplate design from the plate to paper. The paper is pressed against the object to be printed on, dampened and then pulled off. Then the furniture can be polished.

Turning: Producing round objects on a lathe by cutting away wood while the wood revolves.

Undercoat: Layer of chalk or plaster applied to wood as a base for painting or gilding.

Veneer, veneering: Thin sheets of wood with which the blind wood is covered, or the application of veneer to the blind wood.

Vitrine: Shelved case, often mirrored in back, to hold decorative objects.

Walnut: Popular hardwood used in German and French cabinetmaking in the 17th, 18th and 19th centuries. Sawed lengthwise, the usual light brown walnut veneer with blackish graining results. Crosscut, it provides grained veneer with black cloudy patterns. Walnut was usually used as veneer, It bleaches under strong sunlight.

Window sofa: Sofa with angled arms and no back.

Writing bureau: In the late 18th century, a bureau was developed with its uppermost drawer projecting and a down-folding front panel forming a writing surface. Later a small structure with a diagonal writing panel was added instead of the top drawer.

Writing cabinet: Upright secretary or tabernacle secretary with bureau-like or cupboard-like lower part and often gable-crowned top with a closing compartment and drawers. In between, in a central part, equipped with small drawers behind a diagonal cover, which can be folded down as a writing panel. First made in Britain in the early 18th century, it became the most ornate Rococo furniture type in Germany. After 1780-90 the tabernacle secretary was gradually superseded by the folding secretary, which then became the most popular type of Biedermeier writing furniture.

Bibliography

Ausstellungskatalog Kunsthalle Bremen: *Biedermeier,* Bremen 1967.

Bahns, Jörn, Biedermeier-Möbel, *Entstehung ‾ Zentren ‾ Typen,* Munich 1979.

Bangert, Albrecht, *Kleinmöbel aus drei Jahrhunderten, Typen ‾ Stile ‾ Meister,* Munich 1978.

Bauer, M. P., & Ohm, A., *Europäische Möbel von der Gotik bis zum Jugendstil,* 2nd edition, Frankfurt 1981.

Behme, Theda, *Schlichte deutsche Wohnmöbel,* Munich 1928.

Benker, Gertrud, *Bürgerliches Wohnen,* Munich 1984.

Boehm, Max von, *Biedermeier,* Berlin 1911.

Boehmer, Günter, *Bilderbogen aus dem Biedermeier,* Munich 1961.

____, *Die Welt des Biedermeier,* Munich 1968.

Christiani, Franz-Joseph, *Schreibmöbelentwürfe zu Meisterstücken Braunschweiger Tischler aus der 1. Hälfte des 19. Jahrhunderts,* Braunschweig 1979.

Daun, Thomas, *Die Schreiner Kaulbach in Arolsen.*

Dewiel, Lydia, *Möbelstilkunde. Europäische Möbel aus acht Jahrhunderten,* Munich 1980.

Doderer, O., *Biedermeier,* Mannheim 1958.

Dolz, Renate, *Möbelstilkunde,* Munich 1991.

Eckstein, Hans, *Der Stuhl. Funktion ‾ Konstruktion ‾ Form,* Munich 1977.

Egger, Gerhart, *Beschläge und Schlösser an alten Möbeln,* 2nd edition, Munich 1977.

Egger, Hanna, *Herrn Biedermeiers Wunschbild, Ausstellungskataloge des Österreichischen Museums für angewandte Kunst,* Vienna 1978.

Fabiankowitsch, Gabriele, & Witt-Döring, Christian, *Genormte Fantasie. Zeichenunterricht für Tischler 1800-1840.*

Folnesics, Joseph, *Innenräume und Hausrat der Empire- und Biedermeierzeit in Österreich-Ungarn,* Vienna 1917.

Geismeier, Willi, *Biedermeier,* Leipzig 1979.

Gere, Charlotte, *Nineteenth Century Interiors,* London 1992.

Gloag, Julian, *A Short Dictionary of Furniture,* London 1969.

Haaff, Rainer, *Das süddeutsche Biedermeier,* Westheim 1991.

Hart, H., *Chairs,* New York 1977.

Hauser & Ostendorf, *Biedermeiermöbel in Westfalen entdeckt,* Warendorf 1990.

Hayward, Helena, *World Furniture,* London 1965.

Hellwag, Fritz, *Die Geschichte des deutschen Schreinerhandwerkes.*

Herrmann, G., *Das Biedermeier im Spiegel seiner Zeit,* Oldenburg-Hamburg 1965.

Himmelheber, Georg, *Historismus, Jugendstil,* Munich 1973.

____, *Biedermeiermöbel,* Munich 1987.

____, *Deutsche Möbelvorlagen 1800-1900,* Munich 1988.

____, *Kunst des Biedermeier 1815-1835,* Munich 1988.

Hirth, G., *Das deutsche Zimmer,* Munich & Leipzig 1886.

Hölzl, Christoph (ed.), *Interieurs der Goethezeit,* Augsburg 1999.

Holm, Edith, *Stühle. Von der Antike bis zur Moderne,* Munich 1978.

Kalkschmidt, Eugen, *Biedermeiers Glück und Ende,* Munich 1957.

Katalog Niederösterreichischer Ausstellungsverein, *Biedermeier-Ausstellung,* Vienna 1962.

Klatt, Erich, *Konstruktion alter Möbel,* Stuttgart 1977.

Kratz, Anette-Isabell, *Altonaer Möbel,* Hamburg

1988.

Kreisel, Heinrich, & Himmelheber, Georg, *Die Kunst des deutschen Möbels, Vol. 3, Klassizismus ̄ Historismus ̄ Jugendstil,* Munich 1973.

Krüger, Renate, *Biedermeier-Eine Lebenshaltung,* Vienna 1979.

Luthmer, F., *Deutsche Möbel der Vergangenheit, Monographien des Kunstgewerbes,* Leipzig.

____, & Schmidt, R., *Empire und Biedermeier-Möbel aus Schlössern und Bürgerhäusern,* Frankfurt 1923.

Lux, Josef August, *Empire und Biedermeier,* Stuttgart 1930.

Meister, Peter W. & Jedding, Hermann, *Das schöne Möbel im Lauf der Jahrhunderte,* Munich 1966.

Meyer, A. G. & Graul, R., *Tafeln zur Geschichte der Möbelformen,* Leipzig 1902-1920.

Möller, Renate, *Empire- und Biedermeier-Möbel,* Munich 1998.

Müller-Christensen, *Sigrid, Alte Möbel vom Mittelalter bis zum Jugendstil,* 7th edition, Munich 1968.

Museum für Kunsthandwerk, *Möbelbuch,* Frankfurt 1977.

Nagel, Gert K., *Möbel, Battenberg Antiquitäten-Katalog,* Augsburg 1994.

Österreichisches Museum für angewandte Kunst (ed.), *Teetischmodelle aus der Danhauser'schen Möbelfabrik,* Vienna 1989.

Ohm, Anneliese, *Möbel,* Museum für Kunsthandwerk, Frankfurt am Main.

Ottomeyer, Hans, *Biedermeier Glück und Ende . . . die gestörte Idylle 1815 bis 1848,* Munich, 1987.

____, *Zopf- und Biedermeiermöbel,* Katalog des Münchener Stadtmuseums, Munich 1991.

____, & Hofer, Gerhard (ed.), *Die Möbel der Residenz München des Empire, Biedermeier und Spätklassizismus,* Munich-New York 1997.

Ottomeyer & Schlapka, *Biedermeier,* Munich 2000.

Parnass Sonderheft 4/1987, *Das wilde Biedermeier 1800 bis 1848,* Vienna 1987.

Pauls, Eilh. Erich, *Das politische Biedermeier,* Lübeck 1925.

Sangl, Sigrid, *Empire- und Biedermeiermöbel aus der fürstlichen Sammlung Thurn und Taxis,* Weltkunst Vol. 94, No. 22, 1994, pp. 3199-3202.

Schaefer, Veronika, *Leo von Klenze: Möbel und Innenräume. Ein Beitrag zur höfischen Wohnkultur im Spätbiedermeier,* Munich 1980, Monacensia Vol. 89.

Schmidt, Robert, *Möbel.* Bibliothek für Kunst- und Antiquitätensammler, 4th edition, Berlin, 1920.

Schmitz, Hermann, *Festräume und Wohnzimmer des Deutschen Klassizismus und Biedermeier,* Berlin 1920.

____, *Deutsche Möbel des Klassizismus,* Stuttgart 1923.

____, *Das Möbelwerk,* Berlin 1942 & Tübingen 1963.

Schwarze, Wolfgang, *Antike deutsche Möbel,* 2nd edition, Wuppertal 1972.

Sievers, Johannes, *Karl Friedrich Schinkel, Die Möbel,* Berlin 1950.

Stone, Dominic R., *Die grosse Zeit des Biedermeier 1815 bis 1848,* Hamburg 1991.

Suppan, Martin, *Biedermeier-Schreibmöbel,* Vienna 1987.

Thümmler, Sabine, *Die Geschichte der Tapete, Raumkunst auf Papier,* Eurasburg 1998.

Ungern-Sternberg, A, von, *Erinnerungsblätter aus der Biedermeier-Zeit,* Potsdam 1919.

Völker, Angela, *Biedermeier Stoffe, Die Sammlung des MAK Wien,* Munich-New York 1996.

Voltz, Johann Michael, *Bilder aus dem Biedermeier,* Baden-Baden 1957.

Wiese, Wolfgang, *Johannes Klinckerfuss, ein Württembergischer Ebenist,* Sigmaringen 1988.

Wilkie, Angus, *Biedermeier,* New York 1992 & Hildesheim 1996.

Wirth, Irmgard, *Berliner Biedermeier,* Berlin 1972.

Zinnkann, Heidrun, *Mainzer Möbelschreiner der ersten Hälfte des 19. Jahrhunderts,* Frankfurt, 1985.

Zweig, Marianne, *Zweites Rokoko,* Vienna 1924.

Ziegenhorn & Jucker Hoflieferanten, *Rückblick auf die historischen Möbelformen im Zusammenhang mit der modernen Raumkunst,* Erfurt, no year.

Photo Credits

We would like to thank the following dealers and auction houses heartily for making the illustrations available:

Absenger und Musser, AMK Kunsthandel, Fürstenstrasse 10, 80333 Munich: #1, 2, 75, 96, 112, 279, 285, 357, 372, 382, 384, 385, 389, 441, 467, 472, 516, 517, 527, 529, 549.

Andersch Kunsthandel, Weinmarkt 14, 90403 Nuremberg: #139, 141.

Andréewitch, Stephan, Kunsthandel, Favoritenstrasse 10, A-1040 Vienna: #98, 99, 135, 358, 386.

Arne Bruun Rasmussen, Kunstauktionen, Bredgade 33, 1260 Kopenhagen, Denmark: 95, 537.

Arnold, Kunstauktionen, Bleichstrasse 42, 60313 Frankfurt am Main: 29, 51, 177.

Art Domus, Kunsthandel, Mennonitenkirchstrabe 50, 47798 Krefeld: *Kat, Nrn.:* 508, 524, 526.

Art Fundus, Günther und Babanek, Kunsthandel, Utzschneiderstrasse 3, 80469 Munich: #17, 49, 66, 90, 203, 217, 218, 277, 310, 314, 340, 422, 429, 444, 468, 477, 484.

Badum, Kunstauktionen, Karolinenstrasse 11, 96049 Bamberg: #47, 52, 142, 193, 304, 307, 316, 322, 333, 334, 335, 387, 434, 545.

Baumann Regensburg, Kunsthandel, Dr. W. Baumann M.A., Kramgasse 6, 93047 Regensburg: # 398, 411, 449.

Bayerisches Nationalmuseum, Munich: #349.

Bödiger, Kunstauktionen, Franziskanerstrasse 17-19, 53113 Bonn: #452, 456, 505.

Bohm S., Kunsthandel, Marlene Bohm, Barfüsserstrasse 12, und Rohn'sche Badehaus, 37073 Göttingen: #48, 55, 138, 165, 182, 184, 320, 325, 332.

Böhringer, Georg, Kunsthandel, Bergische Landstrasse 509, 40629 Düsseldorf: #30, 35, 43, 46, 174, 194, 268, 269, 391, 432, 489, 521.

Bolland & Marotz, Kunstauktionen, Fedelhören 19, 28203 Bremen: #54, 58, 92, 336.

Breier, Kunsthandel, Bahnhofstrasse 2, 73265 Dettingen/Teck: #355.

Britsch, Kunsthandel, Georg Britsch, Jr., Bahnhofstrasse 135, 88427 Bad Schussenried: #27, 28, 33, 69, 78, 79, 86, 233, 255, 261, 287, 294, 324, 359, 368, 371, 374, 419454, 496, 520, 525.

Coloneum, Kunsthandel, Alwin Homeier, Tändlergasse 2, 93047 Regensburg: #42, 64, 65, 150, 159, 211, 214, 252, 253.

Corpus delicti, Restaurierungen-Kunsthandel, Rosenheimer Strasse 91, 83101 Thansau/Rohrdorf: #154.

Ehrl, Kunsthandel, Nürnberger Strasse 1, Schloss Greding, 91171 Greding: #41, 145, 164, 363, 514.

Hawari, Kunsthandel, Dreimühlenstrasse 16, 80469 München: #89, 102, 103, 104, 105, 131, 136, 228, 260, 301, 407, 474.

Hensoldt, Kunsthandel, Wertherstrasse 29, 35578 Wetzlar: #487.

Jordan, Kunsthandel, Amalienstrasse 14-15, 80333 Munich: $56, 219.

Köhler, Kunsthandel, Hauptstrasse 5, 97332 Volkach: #100, 151, 161, 173, 212, 492.

Lempertz, Kunstauktionen, Neumarkt 3, 50667 Köln: #308, 309, 380, 552, 553, 555.

Lips, Kunsthandel ˉRestaurierungen, Inhaber Hundt, Wiener Platz 8, 81667 Munich: #9, 34, 40, 44, 50, 63, 114, 124, 152, 153, 158, 189, 205, 210, 215, 226, 230, 240, 245, 246, 326, 338a, 347, 405, 427, 445, 458, 470, 538.

Miri, Kunsthandel, Keithstrasse 8, 10787 Berlin: #172.

von Mitzlaff, Kunsthandel, Prinzessinnen-Haus, 63607 Wächtersbach: #186, 187.

Möller, Kunsthandel, Bunsenstrasse 9, 74915 Waibstadt: #157, 546.

Nagel, Kunstauktionen, Adlerstrasse 31-33, 70030 Stuttgart: #3, 4, 7, 8, 12, 21, 22, 23, 26, 53, 57, 59, 60, 67, 68, 73, 74, 80, 81, 82, 84, 85, 87, 88, 91, 94, 95, 108, 109, 110, 111, 113, 118, 119, 126, 132, 134, 146, 147, 155, 166, 168, 170, 178, 179, 180, 181, 183, 185, 204, 207, 208, 216, 221, 222, 223, 224, 225, 227, 229, 234, 236, 237, 238, 239, 251, 258, 265, 267, 270, 271, 272, 273, 276, 280, 281, 284, 288, 290, 291, 298, 299, 302, 303, 305, 306, 315, 319, 327, 328, 329, 339, 342, 343, 352, 354, 362, 364, 365, 369, 370, 381, 392, 394, 395, 396, 410, 412, 414, 416, 418, 421, 436, 437, 451, 462, 463, 464, 465, 466, 469, 473, 481, 493, 495, 498, 499, 501, 506, 507, 509, 510, 512, 513, 515, 518, 519, 528, 530, 532, 533, 534, 535, 536, 539, 542, 543, 547, 554, 556.

Neumeister, Kunstauktionen, Barerstrasse 37, 80799 Munich: #5, 56, 200, 297, 313, 318, 351, 360, 366, 446, 447, 453, 459, 503.

Niederecker, Galerie am Herzogpark, Kufsteiner Platz 5, 81679 Munich: #20, 160, 169, 278, 282, 283, 356, 388, 390, 393, 438, 442, 445.

Private individuals: #6, 24, 93, 97, 125, 133, 140, 143, 144, 235, 243, 266, 274, 275, 314, 321, 367, 408, 415, 478, 482a, 488, 531.

Reisch, Kunsthandel, Meersburger Strasse 24, 88048 Friedrichshafen: #540.

Rosemann, Antiquitäten am Schlossberg, Wasserbergstrasse 41, 91257 Pegnitz: #37, 195, 209, 247, 300, 323, 338, 461, 497.

Ruef, Hugo, Kunstauktionen, Gabelsbergerstrasse 28, 80333 Munich: #123, 129.

Rummel, Kunsthandel, Textorstrasse 13-15, 97070 Würzburg: #378, 379.

Schlapka, Kunsthandel, Gabelsbergerstrasse 9, 80333 Munich: #11, 14, 16, 19, 25, 32, 38, 39, 62, 76, 83, 106, 115, 116, 117, 120, 121, 122, 128, 130, 167, 171, 188, 190, 192, 206, 213, 220, 231, 242, 244, 254, 262, 263, 264, 286, 289, 293, 296, 312, 317, 330, 331, 341, 345, 348, 361, 383, 397, 399, 400, 401,402, 403, 404, 406, 409, 413, 417, 420, 423, 424, 425, 443, 448, 450, 457, 471, 475, 476, 479, 480, 482, 483, 485, 491, 511, 522, 523, 541, 550, 551.

Schloss Ahlden, Kunstauktionen, Schloss, 29691 Ahlden an der Aller: #177, 198, 548.

Schmitz-Avila, Kunsthandel, Koblenzer Strasse 36 & 55, 53498 Bad Breisig: #377.

Semler, Kunsthandel und Sachverständiger, Simpliziusbrunnen 15-17, 36037 Fulda: #15, 61, 70, 71, 72, 232, 256, 292, 295, 337, 375, 376.

Senger, Kunsthandel, Karolinenstrasse 8-10, 96049 Bamberg: #13.

Sotheby's, Kunstauktionen, Odeonsplatz 16, 80539 Munich: #176.

Spik, Kunstauktionen, Kurfürstendamm 66, 10707 Berlin: #163, 197.

Spindler, Kunsthandel, Baaderstrasse 45, 80469 Munich: #10, 137, 311, 373, 435, 440, 486, 490, 502.

Störmer, Kunsthandel, Theresienstrasse 66, 80333 Munich: #18, 428.

Streminski, Kunsthandel, Marienburgerstrasse 13b, 50670 Köln: 433.

Van Ham, Kunstauktionen, Schönhauser Strasse 10-16, 50908 Köln: #127, 148, 149, 156, 162, 196, 199, 201, 202, 241, 257, 346, 350, 353, 460, 500, 504, 544.

Wedell, Kunsthandel, Briennerstrasse 12, 80333 Munich: 31, 36, 101, 426, 439.

Directory of Dealers

Germany

Bad Schussenried	Georg Britsch, Jr., Kunsthandel
Bamberg	Senger Bamberg, Kunsthandel
Berlin	Antiquitätenviertel
Düsseldorf	Kunsthandel Georg Böhringer
Fulda	Kunsthandel Stephan Semler, with Restoration Shop, Appraising
Halfing near Chiemsee	Wolfgang Eller, Kunstsachverständiger
Krefeld	Ars Domus, Almuth Böhm, prop.
Munich	Schlapka KG, Biedermeier Möbel & Gegenwartskunst
Munich	Art Fundus, Biedermeiermöbel
Munich	Dominik Wedell, Antiquitäten, Kunsthandel
Munich	AMK Kunsthandel, Antiquitäten (Biedermeier, Empire)
Munich	Galerie am Herzogpark, Kunst und Möbel des Empire und Biedermeier
Munich	Antiquitäten Hawari, with Restoration Shop
Munich	Antiquitäten Preller, with Restoration Shop, Appraising
Nuremberg	Antiquitäten und Kunstgalerie Johann A. Andersch
Regensburg	Coloneum, Antiquitäten
Rottach-Egern	Antiquitäten am See, Dieter Herbel
Stuttgart	Nagel-Auktionen
Thausen bei Rosenheim	Corpus Delicti, Restoration, Technical Appraisal
Wetzlar	Kunsthandel Hensoldt Biedermeier bis Barock, Möbel und Kunst
Wiesbaden	Regina Schmitz Avila, Kunsthandel

Austria

Vienna	Kunsthandel Stephan Andreewitch